P9-DBK-530

CHOCOLATE

for a

MOTHER'S
HEART

KAY ALLENBAUGH

A FIRESIDE BOOK
Published by Simon & Schuster
New York London Toronto Sydney Singapore

F

FIRESIDE
Rockefeller Center
1230 Avenue of the Americas
New York, NY 10020

Manufactured in China

1   3   5   7   9   10   8   6   4   2

ISBN 0-7432-2243-1

CONTENTS

Contents

III

THE INTUITIVE EDGE

IV

DIVINELY SENT

Contents

V

BETWEEN US GIRLS

MORE CHOCOLATE STORIES?

Do you have a short story you want published that fits the spirit of *Chocolate for a Woman's Soul,* or *Chocolate for a Woman's Blessings?* I am planning future editions using a similar format that will feature love stories, divine moments, overcoming obstacles, following our intuition, and humorous events that teach us to laugh at ourselves. I am seeking heartwarming stories of one to four pages in length that feed and lift the spirit, and encourage us to go for our dreams.

I invite you to join me in these future projects by sending your special story for consideration. If your story is selected, you will be listed as a contributing author, receive a one-time honorarium fee, and have a biographical paragraph about you included. For more information, or to send a story, please contact:

Kay Allenbaugh
P.O. Box 2165
Lake Oswego, Oregon 97035

<kay@allenbaugh.com>

For more information, please visit my Web site!

http://www.chocolateforwomen.com

INTRODUCTION

he inspirational stories you're about to read all deal with motherhood—you'll enjoy them whether you're a mom yourself or simply in need of a little mothering.

Moms have one of the simplest but toughest job descriptions around: Do it all, and then some! We're teachers, friends, chauffeurs, cooks, nurses, stage managers, career counselors, and most of all, safe havens. We need to know when to be there, and when to bite our tongues. We must shelter, guide, and protect—and then at precisely the right moment, push our precious offspring from the nest. Motherhood is a job with more variety than the biggest box of chocolates you can envision! And that's why all the stories in *Chocolate for a Mother's Heart* were written with so many different types of women in mind.

Of course, you don't need to be a mom or need some mothering to understand the double-edged nature of the maternal instinct—women who have a motherly nature always seem to be the ones others depend upon, whether it's at home or in the office, whether it's a child who needs some mothering, a spouse, a best friend, or even our own moms! And because all mothers seem to hold themselves up to such high standards, sometimes they need a little extra nurturing—and indulging—too. That's why the stories in this new "chocolate" book were written to inspire, empower, and delight you.

Chocolate for a Mother's Heart is an extension of my journey after being divinely inspired to write *Chocolate for a Woman's Soul*.

My own mother died young, at age forty, when I was fifteen years old. The enormous loss I've felt over the years has been a constant reminder to me of how irreplaceable mothers really are. But though I miss my mother, I know that she's always been with me in spirit, protecting me as I go through life. Losing Mom has also made me incredibly grateful for all the time I've been given with my children.

With the kind of unconditional love that only a mother can provide—and a reminder that mothers know best—I offer you a variety of deliciously rich, real-life "chocolate stories." So go ahead, indulge in these soul-satisfying treats, and take it from this mom: they will just whet your appetite for more!

I

MILK AND COOKIES

*The journey toward the heart
is always a journey home.*

—Jennifer James, Ph.D.

A child does not thrive on what [she] is prevented from doing,
but on what [she] actually does.
—Marcelene Cox

A DIFFERENT PERSPECTIVE

hen my daughter Adrienne was twelve years
old, she took a photography class. She informed me
that real photographers use black-and-white film. I
agreed. We bought the film and she decided to take pictures of
the St. Louis Gateway Arch.

The day was overcast. I recommended we wait for sun, but
she thought the light optimal for the photograph she envisioned.
The minute we got to the arch, Adrienne walked up to one of
the massive triangular-shaped legs, arched her entire body backwards against it, arms stretched overhead, and pointed her camera straight up the side.

I said in my most caring, motherly voice, "Honey, you need to
back up and get the entire arch in the picture." Anyone who has
ever seen a photo of the arch knows what I mean. "It won't
make sense if you can't see the entire thing," I said.

She ignored me and moved to the other leg, repeating her position. I tried again to tell her the best way to take the picture. I
wanted her to get a good photograph, but she was clearly unim-
pressed by my sage advice and years of experience snapping
birthday parties, dance recitals, and vacations.

"No, I want to do it this way," she said.

I thought, okay, we'll waste a little money on film and developing, but she'll learn her lesson.

It turns out I learned the lesson. Years later, Adrienne won a scholarship from the San Francisco Art Institute, interned at Ansel Adams Center for Photography, and had a show at the Museum of Modern Art in San Francisco. People buy her photographs because she has a unique vision. A vision that spurred her at twelve to photograph the Gateway Arch from an angle I thought would never work.

The way my daughter approached that photo taught this mother that most solutions we need are right in front of us—if we are willing to look at an opportunity with a new and different perspective.

Thank goodness Adrienne didn't see the arch through my lens. That photo has been purchased by collectors and now hangs in several galleries.

LINDA NASH

We are rich only through what we give,
and poor only through what we refuse.
—ANNE-SOPHIE SWETCHINE

THE RARE MONGOLIAN RABBIT

*P*erhaps the frequency with which it so often happens nowadays should have lessened the pain; misery does love company, after all. But hearing that my husband's job would be "phased out" was unforgettable and shocking.

John, my husband of ten years, expressed his concern over this nightmare occurrence. He assured me that he would do everything possible to get a job to provide for our family. With three children under the age of five and one due very shortly, we relied on his income entirely.

"Life goes on," John said, more outwardly upbeat than I over the situation. "We have our health, and after all, it's only a job. Besides, the company will continue paying me for three more months. I'll surely have a new job by then. Just relax and don't worry."

With his excellent university and professional credentials, I figured he must be right. He was a former Olympic athlete and knew about taking on a challenge. His father died when John was young, so he took on the responsibility of keeping his mother, sister, and brother together. My husband knew how to work hard and smart. But as the months passed and no job possibilities materialized for him, I grew more and more fearful and less "faith-abiding." What if he couldn't find a job? Under other circumstances I could have returned to classroom teaching, but our fourth child was due in less than three months.

With little money in our savings account, the mortgage payment two months behind, and no possible income from any other source, I whittled away at our daily-living budget.

Eventually our food budget became almost nonexistent. One day while in the supermarket with my children, I noticed a young box boy packing overly ripe fruit and outdated food into cardboard boxes. Hesitantly, I inquired about the destination of the food. "We sell it real cheap, and whatever isn't sold is thrown away," he said. I eyed the aging carrots, celery, tomatoes. Food we could use for weeks. What, I wondered, is the proper etiquette for begging for food for one's children?

"We have a rare Mongolian rabbit!" I heard myself blurt out, glancing at my three hungry children. "I'd be interested in purchasing the food for the rabbit."

He replied easily, "Since it's just a rabbit, there won't be any charge."

That day he loaded five boxes of produce into my car. We talked while he worked, me sharing information about my soon-to-be-expanding family and him talking about his. His name was Jeff. I learned he came from a family of five where finances were tight. This job helped pay for his college education.

Weeks went by, and Jeff began packing the boxes with outdated or damaged items—peanut butter, soup, and cheese—that were otherwise still good but would be thrown away. "Surely a rare rabbit would eat all these items," he said, explaining their inclusion. As the weeks turned into months, we discovered, hidden under the produce, laundry detergent, milk, juice, butter . . . the list goes on and on. Jeff started phoning me every time he had a box of "rabbit food" ready. Now and then, he brought the boxes to our home. He never inquired after the rabbit, content instead to leave its food and be on his way.

When our fourth daughter was born, my elation was tinged with worry about our financial future. "O Lord, please," I begged. "You promised you would never give us more than we can handle. What do you want us to do? Help!"

My husband slipped into the hospital room and said, "I have good news and sad news. The good news is that this morning I've been offered a very exciting job." I closed my eyes and thanked God for his many blessings. "The sad news," he continued, "is that the rare Mongolian rabbit is gone."

It turned out Jeff no longer worked at the supermarket. While I'd been busy with the birth of our new baby, he had moved, the manager said, and left no forwarding address.

Over the next ten years I made good on my silent promise to repay the kindness of all who had helped us throughout that difficult time. But my thanks were incomplete. Then one day, a decade later, there was Jeff standing in the store's office. I noticed the title MANAGER on his name badge.

How does one adequately thank the person who offers assistance without compromising your pride, extends a hand without sapping your strength, and believes in the rare Mongolian rabbits hiding somewhere in each of our lives? I'm not surprised Jeff's risen up the ranks. He has a rare gift. He knew how to listen loudly to my special plea.

"Mrs. Nunn!" he exclaimed, "I think of you and your family often. How is the rabbit?" he inquired softly.

Taking Jeff's hands into mine, I whispered with a wink, "Thanks for asking. The rabbit moved on long ago, and we couldn't be better."

MAUREEN NUNN

ADVENTURES IN GRANDPARENTING

I *had a date with my five-year-old grandson to do some* spring skiing in the California mountains at Bear Lake. I couldn't wait to wrap my arms around that boy and look into his smiling eyes. I'd taken him on his inaugural ski adventure some months before. He had hung on to that tow rope for dear life, and then spent most of his time bouncing and sliding his way down the bunny hill. No matter how he got to the bottom, once there he would throw his arms up to the sky in jubilation. I remember saying to him, "Justin, what I like best about you is that you don't give up!"

Before flying to California for our next special time together, I introduced Justin to the notion that you can "set an intention" for just about anything you want to do, and make it happen in spite of the obstacles. After talking on the phone several times before the trip, we decided on our intention: To have a fun and grand adventure together—no matter what. I told him to picture that in his mind over and over again, and I would do the same.

I picked him up on a glorious sunny morning. "You know, there's just one possible little snag that we need to talk about," I said to Justin as we started our drive toward the mountain. "Last night, El Niño blew through and dumped eight inches of fresh powder on these mountains. The ski conditions are going to be great, but the road conditions might be tricky. There might be too much ice and snow on the road for this rental car to make it, because I don't have any chains."

True, we didn't have chains, and I didn't want to buy any. Why buy chains when I've never ever successfully put chains on a car? Justin turned to me, gave me his big, knowing smile, and said, "Let's go, Grandma!" So onward we climbed, gradually making our way up the mountain pass. We came around a bend, and the first challenge to our intention confronted us. Ice! Not just a little patch, but ice on the road as far as you could see.

Eight cars had pulled over, and a body was sticking out from below each one as these drivers attempted to put on their chains. Friends and family offered encouragement and advice to those contorted under their cars. Not a pretty sight. I found myself thinking quickly about alternative ways to entertain Justin.

"Well, Justin," I said, "this may be a challenge for us." Just as I was about to say, "Hey, how about we turn back and go see a movie instead?" Justin piped up. "You know, Grandma, what I like best about us is that we don't give up." Why did that sound so familiar? We were definitely at a decision point when I remembered that the intention of this trip was to be an adventure. And *anything* can happen on an adventure.

Buoyed by his confidence, I turned back to the market we had passed ten miles back to see if they had chains. Still feeling a need to point out the practical side of things, I said, "Now, there's no guarantee that they will have any chains, and there's no guarantee that I'm going to be able to get them on the car. I've never been able to do it before." Justin responded simply, "Let's go see, and then we'll ask God for help." He put his hands together, and with all the faith in his tiny body, he prayed, "Dear God, please help my grandma put on the chains, and if she can't, send a man." What a great idea! My excitement mounted as we confronted the second challenge to our intention of having a grand adventure together—no matter what.

With lightning speed, the guy at the market sold us chains to fit the rental car, and we were back on the road. Approaching the familiar icy curve, I slowed down, ready to pull in behind a line of cars like the one we'd seen on our first attempt up the mountain. As we rounded the bend, no one was there. Lots of ice, but not a car to be seen.

My heart sank as the third challenge to having a great adventure presented itself. Once again, Justin focused on our goal as I focused on the obstacles. Just as I was about to prepare my grandson for the inevitable, he said it again: "The thing I like best about us, Grandma, is that we don't give up." So, of course, I had to give it a shot. And I did. And I failed. *Time to go home and find a movie,* I said to myself as I struggled fruitlessly with the heavy chains. Then, I heard a voice say, "Ma'am, can I help you?" I turned around and faced a John Wayne look-alike. Moments later, with chains in place, we were on our way again.

Several miles later, I heard the unmistakable thud of chains coming undone. It seemed like the forces were against us as the fourth challenge to our intention surfaced—before we'd even reached the ski slopes. Fresh out of ideas, I muttered under my breath, "Set an intention, picture it over and over—no matter what." Within moments of my pulling over, a man stopped his pickup, hopped out, grabbed his tools, and tightened the chains. I didn't even need to ask him for assistance. Maybe the Force was with us after all.

The day became one Disney moment after another. The hills were alive with the sound of music as we sang "Banana, bo-bana" while racing down the slopes. The brook was babbling. The sun was shining and Justin was skiing powder—a grand adventure—just as we intended!

Exhausted and exhilarated at the end of a glorious day, we loaded our skis and boots back into the car and I slid behind the wheel. My grandson, this five-year-old bundle of joy seated next to me, looked up at me with his radiant eyes. Confidently he said, "Grandma, you know what I like best about us?"

REV. MARY OMWAKE

FAMILY SCENTS

My *Aunt Esther loved children, all of them. When* she realized she would never have a child of her own, she wisely followed her heart and became a teacher. Outside the classroom, when she wasn't gardening or canning, she entertained and taught the other children in her life. Fortunately, my sister and I were among the lucky ones.

We adored her, and why not? She let us do darn near anything. We could turn any room into a fort, build a seawall in the bathtub, or create weird science experiments in the kitchen. She played the part of the ringmaster as our imaginations ran wild! I remember her as magical, perhaps partly because of the way she smelled. She favored a pine-scented soap that seemed to permeate the air with a hint of tingling, almost mystical energy.

I admit I failed to recognize her real gifts until I grew older. In reflection, I imagine the true beauty of my aunt's spirit came from her refusal to use the word "mistake" or "failure" in the presence of a child. In her eyes we could do anything or become anyone, and because of that belief in us, many times we did!

Years later, my sister and I had our own children, and they too got to experience the "magic" of a visit to Aunt Esther's house. As babies, each one of the six children sat in her sunny dining nook and tried to catch sunbeams as they streamed in from a window smudged with handprints. Regardless of how many children she'd witnessed do the same, she always exclaimed, "Now, that's a remarkable child. Look, he's [or she's] already fascinated with the mystery of nature."

I think the weekend one of the girls pretended to be a "doggy" best illustrates this kind woman's patience and willingness to encourage imagination. Little Jennifer spent three days running around the house on her hands and knees. Barely speaking, she chose instead to bark or whine her needs to Aunt Esther. "Why, she even allowed her to eat out of dishes on the floor," my father remarked with a shake of his head.

Throughout the years, she taught generations of children everything from the joy of feeding ducks in the front-yard ponds to the more refined appreciation of literature. I'll always treasure the rainy afternoons we spent in her living room listening to her read from a poetry book or one of the classics.

When she died, she left us quietly, with dignity and grace. We were all comforted by the knowledge that she spent her final days surrounded by family and friends. It served as a fitting farewell to a woman who gave so much.

Considering all the wondrous moments she created on earth, it shouldn't come as a surprise to learn she still works her magic from beyond. A few sensitive souls in my family get an occasional visit from Aunt Esther; we call them "scentings."

I'll never forget the day my sister called to tell me about "the most amazing thing that just happened." She'd smelled the unmistakable scent of our aunt's soap and noticed an indentation on a freshly made bed. A bed that once belonged to Aunt Esther. In addition, my sister says, she was overcome with feelings of peace and love.

A couple of the older kids, the ones who once played at her feet years ago, also tell stories of awakening from a fitful sleep to a scent of pine and a feeling that their great-aunt is watching over them. Even my mother has experienced a "scenting" or two. "Especially," she says, "when I'm mulling over an issue or worried about one of the children." It's no accident, I'm sure, that my aunt visits when one of us is in need of a little extra faith or love.

Many evenings, I sit in quiet solitude and think of her. There's little sadness in remembering, since all my memories of her fill my heart with smiles and joy. Every now and again, in the still night air, she sits with me. I sense the tingle and smell the pine, while I imagine the lined and loving face of the woman who wore it well.

DEBB JANES

A LONG WAY FROM HOME

*T*he year was 1947. My parents loaded the car with suitcases while I looked for my elusive tomcat, Snoonie, to say goodbye. I was excited to be vacationing in my favorite place in the whole world—Atlantic City: cotton candy, saltwater taffy, the steel pier, the beach, and all the ocean a ten-year-old could want.

Calling for him, I entered the woods behind my house to search the wild apple orchard and his blackberry patch hideout. I never figured out why we chose that name for a cat. A family epithet, I was told. No matter. I loved him, and I knew in cat language that he loved me. I had no siblings, and Snoonie was my tolerant confidant. I told him everything.

Sure enough, he sauntered out from under a ripe berry bush, stretching and mewing at me for having disturbed his summer nap. I cradled him in my arms and said, "Time to go on vacation, but you have to stay here. I wish you could come with me, but they don't allow cats or dogs at the motel." I scratched between his ears until I heard his soft, rhythmic purr and whispered, "Be good for Janet and her mom. And no leaving mice at their front door with the morning paper. And don't beg food from the men building the house across the street." I kissed the little black circle atop Snoonie's head. "See you in three weeks," I said, and situated him beneath the bush again.

It was early September when we returned from Atlantic City. I jumped from the car and began calling for Snoonie. I combed the woods, shouting his name. There was no sign of him. An ominous feeling was growing in the pit of my stomach as I raced to my friend Janet's house, only to discover my beloved cat had been missing for a week. Janet and her mother had checked the entire neighborhood, while keeping bowls of fresh cat food at the door. I pushed the horror of squished road cats from my mind and kept telling myself that Snoonie would turn up.

One afternoon a workman from the crew across the street waved me over.

"Little girl," he said, "I hear you calling for Snoonie every day. Is that a dog or a cat, or what?"

"It's my cat. He's a black-and-white boy cat with a circle atop his head. We left on vacation for three weeks, and now he's gone." I tried to hold back welling tears, but they overflowed and ran down my cheeks.

The workman removed his cap and scratched his head, thinking. "Black and white, you say. Yeah, there was a cat like that hanging around here. One of the guys used to feed him tuna from his lunch box. When his plumbing job was over, and no one had claimed the cat, he thought it was a stray and took it home with him."

"Where does he live?" I exclaimed with relief. "I'll tell my dad and we'll drive to the man's house and get Snoonie back."

"I can't help you there, little girl," the workman said, shaking his head. "All I know is the man's name is Frank and he lives in the city—miles away from here."

I went home crying. My parents questioned the workman again, even called the contractor supervising the job, but he didn't have any information on Frank. Then they sat me down to tell me the words I didn't want to hear—my Snoonie was gone. "We'll get you another kitty," my mother said in an attempt to cheer me up. I didn't want another cat. I wanted Snoonie back.

When winter had blanketed our house with snow that fell hard and heavy, I would sit on the sofa overlooking the window-sill where Snoonie used to perch. Though he wasn't with me, I remembered him in my prayers, asking God to please bring him back.

One unforgettable night, while on the sofa, I saw a flicker of movement. I glanced out at the sill and saw a very bedraggled and scrawny black-and-white cat. I started yelling, "Snoonie! Snoonie!" Somehow, my brave cat had come home to his family. We were overjoyed to see him and immediately set out to fatten him up.

Days later, there was a knock at our door. It was a stranger, a man who introduced himself as Frank. My father invited him in. Frank said he had run into the contractor and heard our story. Then he apologized for taking our cat home with him. He said he would have returned the cat, but that Snoonie was now missing from his house and he was afraid the cat had been run over by busy traffic. My dad laughed and said, "Wait until you see this!" He took Frank to the dining room heating vent, where Snoonie was curled up sleeping on his blanket.

"I can't believe my eyes," Frank said, bending down to scratch Snoonie's black circle. We told him the date our cat had returned and how emaciated he looked. "It's a miracle," Frank remarked. "I figure he was traveling for about two months. I live in the city, some thirty-five miles from here." He smiled down at my contented, purring cat and said, "I guess he took the long way home."

JOAN ROELKE

BABY MARK

My son-in-law and I had spent three restless days in my daughter's 12-foot-by-12-foot labor room. Shortly before midnight her doctor gave up on a natural delivery and prepared us for a cesarean birth. When I asked if I might still be able to see my grandchild come into the world, I was told that there was only room for the father in the surgical suite. The doctor encouraged my son-in-law to take a quick break while they prepared my daughter for surgery. He did so, but on his way back to the suite, the elevator he rode in became stuck between floors! The nurses dressed me instead to go into the operating room.

I arrived just as the doctor made the incision in my daughter's belly. I took a seat beside her head. She was sedated yet fully conscious, and her disappointment that her husband wasn't there soothing her between contractions was understandable.

As the nurse held the baby up for my daughter to see, he turned from a pink-tinted blue to gray. His little head flopped over. Heartache and pain overwhelmed me, but I managed to keep stroking my daughter's head, telling her about the baby's long black hair and how beautiful he looked. The nurse confirmed my fears when I heard her say, "Breathe, baby, breathe." My daughter's breath quickened, and she stretched to see past the sheet draped to block our view.

"Your baby is very sick," the nurse said as she scooped my grandson up and ran for the back corridor leading into the intensive care unit. Halfway down the corridor she turned, looked at me and said, "Are you coming?" Me in ICU? Absolutely not. The ache in my heart weighted me to the plastic orange chair. I couldn't bear to bond with this child knowing he might not live. I turned to my daughter. "Do you want me to go with the baby?" She sank back into the bed, closed her eyes, and nodded yes.

Three doctors and six nurses worked on my grandson in the ICU. They motioned me to come near, but I refused. As this new-born clung to life on a ventilator, nurses inserted more tubes and lovingly patted him. "Come on, baby," they said. "Come on."

Finally something inside me burst. "His name is *Mark!*" I shouted. The staff paused and looked at me. I felt as small as the baby. Monitors ticked, whirred, and bleeped. "Keep moving," someone said, and their frenetic pace resumed. Early in her pregnancy, I remembered my daughter mentioning six names, including Mark. Nurses wrote "Mark" on all my grandson's instruments, and it cemented my connection with him that I knew I wouldn't lose no matter what.

With as much compassion as possible, the doctors gave me a blow-by-blow prognosis. Mark's lungs were filled with fluid, he couldn't breathe on his own, they suspected heart problems and the possibility of spinal meningitis. "Pray," a doctor told me. Although I have always loved God, I didn't hold much hope after the doctors' diagnosis. I'd known of many mothers and grand-mothers who'd prayed their most sincere prayers, only to lose their babies.

With my son-in-law now at my daughter's side, they wheeled her bed into the ICU, and the doctors repeated the prognosis. She turned to me and said, "Mom, he's going to be okay, isn't he?" I'd always made everything okay for my daughter, and she needed to hear me say he would be all right, but I couldn't lie. Although my response was noncommittal, I tried to reassure her.

Moments later, out of nowhere, my daughter sat straight up and with great conviction and passion called out, "Mom, he's going to make it! I know he is!" She described a loving presence in the room that surrounded her and suddenly embraced me as well. We both knew this dear baby would be fine.

Within a few hours, my grandson began breathing on his own. Each time I left my daughter's room to check on him, another tube had been removed. He drank his first feeding in two gulps, and his doctor had to be consulted to see if he could have another bottle. A nurse came to announce the good news. "Mark has stabilized," she told us with a big smile.

Oops . . . I realized in all the excitement, I forgot to tell her! My daughter, with a puzzled look on her face, turned to the nurse and asked, "Who's *Mark?*"

JUDITH MCCLURE

A BOUNTIFUL HARVEST

When our first daughter arrived, I didn't hesitate a minute to leave a successful business career to devote myself full-time to making a warm, loving home for our new family. As the years moved on, I never regretted that decision. I genuinely enjoyed my life as a wife, homemaker, and mother. Besides the obvious warm fuzzies of creating a satisfying marriage and cuddling the babies, home life held additional rewards for me. I became an accomplished painter, plasterer, carpenter, and fix-it handyperson. Repeated relocations, due to my husband's career, transformed me into an expert packer and expediter. My artistic talents emerged as I sewed clothes for the children and accessorized one home after another.

Fifteen years later, the life course I had chosen took an abrupt about-face when I had to return to the business world and recreate my ability to earn a living outside the home. Despite long-term counseling, communication with my husband had evaporated and our marriage crumbled. Our lives, headed in different directions, resulted in a long-drawn-out and very difficult divorce.

Not quite fully recovered from the divorce, I struggled terribly with the demands of being a single parent of three active children. Two teenagers and a nine-year-old managed to keep me forever working. Stretching available funds to extraordinary lengths became a daily contest. Haunted by guilt, I watched the children do without so much because I just couldn't afford the extras anymore.

To provide sufficient one-on-one time and moral support for each of the children became my most difficult challenge as a single parent. Time conflicts were all too common. My cheerfulness, energy, and self-esteem eroded daily. Although I had always been a loving, nurturing parent, I started second-guessing my parenting abilities: Am I being too strict, too lenient? Am I giving each child enough attention? Am I setting a good example? Most important, are the children learning the values I want so much to impart to them? Do they feel my love? I felt like a failure.

My oldest daughter, usually a very quiet and private teen, had joined the drama club at school and started acting. This new aspect of her personality surprised and delighted me. The night of her premiere performance, I sat in the front row. Unable to afford roses from a florist, I made her a lovely bouquet of mixed flowers tied together with a rainbow of ribbons.

When the play ended and the cast lined up across the stage for their initial bows, my son ran up and handed his sister the flowers. She positively glowed with happiness and excitement. Yet when the curtains closed and then reopened for the cast's individual bows, she reappeared without the bouquet. I convinced myself that she was disappointed she hadn't received roses as some of the other actresses had. Feeling I'd let her down one more time, tears filled my eyes. Then I noticed that the supporting actresses all appeared with small bunches of flowers cradled in their arms. Now the tears really streamed down my cheeks as I realized my daughter had broken apart her bouquet so that all her friends had flowers to carry on stage for the final applause.

In one wonderful moment, her small act of kindness—like magic—provided the affirmation my sagging spirit needed. She had learned to do more with less. She had come through the pain of divorce okay. So would her brother and sister. And so would I.

PATRICIA KULZER

THELMA SAVES LOUISE

simply didn't want to adopt two little fur balls. It had only been seven weeks since Shauna, my tortoiseshell cat, my wonderful friend and companion, died. For seventeen years she had comforted me through life's ups and downs with no judgment. That cat knew all my secrets and never told anyone. She loved me unconditionally, and I her.

I rescued her from an animal shelter in Green Bay, Wisconsin. The moment I picked her up, I knew she belonged with me. She put one paw around each side of my neck, buried her head into me, and purred. I'm really not sure who picked whom. While I was still grieving that huge loss, my friend Linda showed up at my door with two kittens. "They have nowhere else to go! Look at their cute little faces. Please, you have to save them, Joanne." I felt torn, not ready for a new cat—let alone two—yet agreeing halfheartedly that I would take them in.

I woke up the next morning to two frisky little beings jumping all over me, wide-eyed, wondering why I didn't hurry up and play with them. I flashed on Shauna, who right about now would have been curled up at my side, wondering why I didn't just go back to sleep. I looked right in the faces of these two creatures, knowing we were destined to spend years together and questioned, *How did this happen? And who are you two?*

It didn't take long for those magical bonds to form. I named these feisty critters Thelma and Louise. They'd never take the place of Shauna, but they both wormed their way deeper and deeper into my heart until I couldn't imagine life without them.

Early one morning about six months later, I gathered my things together, ready to head to work. I said goodbye to Louise and turned to say goodbye to Thelma when I noticed her behaving very strangely. I walked into the kitchen to take a closer look. She was in the corner meowing, jumping up and down, and batting at something on the wall. I had never seen her act this way before. "Thelma, what are you doing?" She ignored me and continued to meow and bat at the wall. I looked at where she was hitting and felt the surface. Hotter than an iron! Red hot! I slid my hand up the wall and as I got near the outlet, my hand started to burn. *A fire! Oh, my God! There's a fire in the wall!*

Five minutes later, two firemen were swinging an ax through my kitchen wall, putting out an electrical fire that had started in the wiring. I kept looking over at Thelma thinking, *How did you know?*

Afterward, one of the firemen looked at me and said, "It's a good thing you called when you did. If you had left for work, I'm afraid your house would no longer be standing here."

After he left, I just stood there, holding my two kitties and looking at the hole in the wall. I kissed Thelma again and again and told her what a good cat she'd been. Too busy for words of praise, she jumped from my arms and immediately became enthralled with an emery board she found on the floor, flipping it in the air, grabbing it, carrying it in her mouth as if she were a lioness with her prey.

Both she and Louise like to snuggle up and lick me at the end of the day. Both have earned a great big place in my heart, right along with Shauna.

When I finally did go into work, news of my tale spread like wildfire (pardon the pun). Everyone knew Thelma was a hero. Later that day I checked my mailbox and found that one of my coworkers had dropped off a cartoon. It showed a jet plane about to go down in flames with a poodle at the wheel. "FiFi saves the day!"

Being our savior hasn't gone to Thelma's head. She continues to attack emery boards, likes to walk along the edge of the bathtub—only occasionally falling in—and attacks my toes when I move them under the covers.

I thought I'd saved them by taking them in, but in reality—they saved me.

JOANNE MCCALL

II
MOMS KNOW BEST

Biology is the least of what makes someone a mother.

—Oprah Winfrey

THE TIES THAT BIND

When our son, Rick, told us he planned to marry Amy, my husband and I were ecstatic. A playful, loving couple in their twenties, these two rock-and-roll musicians could not have had more in common—including two doting mothers.

With the wedding a year away, we combined resources with Amy's mom so that the two young lovers might have their perfect wedding.

Weddings call for all the important people in the bride and groom's life to be present. Although both of them are high-functioning beings in the world, they also carry unwanted baggage. Family life and logistics are complicated for kids of divorce.

Rick's dad had left fifteen years before, moving to another state to marry the "other" woman. I married Eric four years later. Rick's feelings of abandonment because his dad simply wasn't around fueled a continual guilty reaction from his father, who claimed all Rick wanted when they talked was money. Infrequent contact over the years punctuated a wilted relationship. Amy's dad was an absentee parent altogether. Although he lived in the same city, she had not seen her father in fourteen years, but she yearned to be loved by him.

Amy worked up the courage to write her dad a letter about six months before the wedding. She introduced herself, told him who she had become, and welcomed his response. He wrote back praising her accomplishments but did not suggest they get together.

The bride-to-be personally designed and engraved her wedding invitations and sent one to her father as well. Rick's dad responded that he wouldn't be attending because his name was not included on the invitation. Rick was disappointed but not really surprised. Amy came home from work one day and was overcome with emotion by the voice she heard on her answering machine. "Amy, this is your dad. I'd be honored to be at your wedding." Another reminder of the lopsided world of divorce.

We rented out the bed-and-breakfast for a day and a half. The wedding ceremony would take place in the living area and the bride and groom, aunts, uncles, sisters, and brothers could stay the night in the rooms upstairs. The majestic historic landmark with its period furniture, rich mahogany moldings, butter-yellow living room, and bronze and crystal chandeliers set the stage for Amy's elegant taste to emerge. To offset her ivory gown, Amy asked the groomsmen to wear dark suits, and her attendants to each wear a long, black dress of their choice. Berries, dried hydrangeas, and fall leaves were secured together by copper-colored ribbons for the exquisite bouquets.

Trees showed off their fall colors on the crisp, sunny wedding day. The front door of the bed-and-breakfast was swung wide open so that guests could file in easily. I recognized Amy's dad immediately from how her mom had described him. I knew that Amy longed to be escorted by her father from the dressing room along the outside walkway of the bed-and-breakfast up to the porch, where she would make a grand entrance through the front door. With her mom's blessing, I asked him. He seemed nervous but anxious to please.

When the beautiful bride and her dad walked into the foyer, she stopped and nuzzled his neck before letting go of his arm. She then walked toward Rick and took a few short inhales—more like audible sobs from a bride on emotional overload.

All was not serious at this wedding, however. Rick and Amy wanted to choose who would perform the ceremony. They

didn't want to have a particular religious denomination repre-
sented, so they selected a clergyman who had received his credentials from a mail-order ad in *Rolling Stone*. At the wedding, the
general consensus was that the minister's lights were not on. Our
suspicions were confirmed when, at the end of the ceremony, he
introduced the newlyweds as "Mrs. and Mrs." Rick Bain.

When Amy's mom graciously allowed Amy's dad to play an
important part in the ceremony, and he rose to the occasion,
Amy was allowed to heal a lifetime of hurts. When Rick was able
to let go of his wish that his father be present, he was able to
focus on the hundred people present who loved him and wished
them well. They created and pulled off their perfect wedding in
an imperfect world.

After a lively reception, followed by dinner, the bride and
groom decided to call it a night and they headed to their room.
About ten minutes later, Amy's mom and I got word from the
innkeeper that the bride and groom wanted to say good night.
So we knocked gently at their door and walked into the bridal
suite, dimly lit by antique lamps.

The newlyweds, wrapped up in white terry-cloth bathrobes
provided by the bed-and-breakfast, were lying under the covers,
grinning from ear to ear. In their eyes, we saw another opportunity for love and happiness to blossom.

Like two mother bears, bound by our devotion to our cubs,
we walked to the head of the bed, leaned over and tucked our
kids in, then symbolically traded sides and tucked again—forever
sealing those ties that bind.

KAY ALLENBAUGH

SAM'S PURPOSE

or years now, I have held the hands of the dying. "How can you bear it?" people ask me. "Hospice nursing must be so difficult. How can you stand to be around so much suffering?" Those people don't understand that if you have the courage to look beyond suffering, you find strength. If you have the forbearance to tackle deformity, you encounter triumph. I know this for a fact. Sam taught me.

An unlikely teacher, this infant of mine. The one the pediatrician said I couldn't take home from the hospital after his birth. Disappointment had struck me then, as a new twenty-year-old mother, but fear lodged in me when the doctor mentioned serious problems and the need for more tests. Shock and disbelief gripped me when he predicted Sam would not improve. When I found a small voice to ask what we could do now, he seemed almost irritated at my lack of comprehension. As if to settle the matter once and for all, he blurted, "Your baby is severely retarded. He will probably never roll over, never sit, never crawl, never walk or talk." Then, returning to an attempt at advising with compassion, he said, "You're young and healthy. You can have more children. You should begin to think of institutional placement for him." I stopped listening, turned, and walked a few feet toward my hospital bed. I pulled the curtain between me and the world and began to cry as quietly as I could. I looked at the waiting baby layette beside me and began to sob harder.

For the first week I returned every day to stand and stare silently through the nursery window, longing to hold and comfort that baby and myself. Afterward I left and cried for hours more. I woke up every night ready to shake the nightmare, only to feel the more helpless reality. But by the beginning of the second week, I began to feel myself steeling. I stopped crying and did not cry about anything for a very long time. Sam needed me.

My little boy, stricken with cerebral palsy and severe sight and hearing impairments, came home to me after one month. Sam's life has not passed easily. Crayons never seemed a natural fit in his hand. The sound of the ice cream truck never reached his ears to cheer him on a summer day. No one ever chose him to play on the kickball teams hastily thrown together in the street by the neighborhood kids. Yet he has triumphed over every one of the predictions, the imposed limitations dropped upon him by a medical community lacking faith in the spirit of one small boy. With countless hours of therapy sessions, love, encouragement—and mostly his own unbelievable motivation—he learned to speak, read, write, and at age nine walk on his own. And interestingly, as Sam learned to walk, I discovered my independence. As he learned to speak, I too found my voice. The first time he made a joke and a stranger laughed heartily, I discovered the unblemished joy of a life—any life!—well lived.

Because of Sam, I needed to hurry to find the spirited person within myself that I had never seen before. That kind of purpose and spirit has carried me through a humiliating divorce, a number of moves, college, and a career in hospice nursing. It has given me the courage to change my life from one of sterile comfort to one of rich love. Sam needed someone to respond, stand, and speak for him. He needed someone to begin to turn the world right side up again.

That day in the nursery, thirty-three years ago, I knew that he trusted me to do it, so I became that person. With my baby's support, I became the mother he needed. In the process, I also became the woman I always wanted to be.

LINDA RAY

My mother phones daily to ask, "Did you just try to reach me?"
When I reply, "No," she adds, "So, if you're not too busy,
call me while I'm still alive," and hangs up.
—Erma Bombeck

DEAREST LAST-BORN

On May 2, 1926, my parents got married, a condition in which they remained for over sixty-seven years. For the last fifteen of those years, they spent six months a year arguing in Florida and six months a year arguing in New York. During the Florida phase, my mother loved for me to write to her, but because of my busy travel and lecture schedule, I'm rarely in a position to do that, since it's impossible to write and drive at the same time. Therefore, I usually call her on the phone. This is the response to one of my phone calls:

> *Dearest Sweetheart,*
> *It was a pleasure hearing your voice, but your letters give me a bigger thrill, because I read and re-read them. I'm looking forward to seeing you and the kids. How are they doing in school and at home? The movie sounded interesting. Where did you eat? We love you very much. Kiss the kids for us.*
>
> *Just Dad and Me*

Now I ask you, is that a humble person? "Just Dad and Me." That's like getting an eviction notice signed "Just the Landlord."

In any event, how could I deprive my wonderful mother of a letter for her to read and reread? So I wrote her a letter, and here is her response:

> *Dearest Last born,*
>
> *It's really a marvelous thing for a daughter to get a minute's time to write after a two month vacation. I can't understand what you are doing at the senior citizen's. What do you teach them? At this stage of life, I would think you could take lessons from them! I'm glad you had that article to send me, otherwise I don't think I would even have gotten the letter yet. Anyway, I love you and I'm happy to hear that you are enjoying life. Please, please continue! Give my kids a big hug and kiss for me.*
>
> *Love from Dad and Me*

Well, now I decided I could write her a long letter, which I did. I called to tell her I had just sent her the longest letter I had ever written, and she was never going to complain again. Right? Wrong! Here is the answer to my longest letter:

> *Dear Joyce,*
>
> *Yes, your letter was a nice long one. But a letter is a letter, and you only used one stamp, so that means it is only one letter. Come on kid, you will have to write again, and soon. Trying to get you on the phone is a great big joke. Do you ever get off? I have tried a half dozen times and the line was busy, and the other time I got the machine. Forget it. You call me. I will give you back whatever the cost is.*
>
> *Love from Dad and Me*

And now for la pièce de résistance. I was looking for a long hooded fur jacket to keep me warm, because my lectures take me to some of the coldest parts of the country in the dead of winter. I searched for a jacket, checking all the furriers in Hartford and New Haven, but I couldn't afford anything they had. Finally, in desperation, I thought of the old family furrier. I called my mother in Florida and said, "Mom, is Mr. Walowitz in Brooklyn still in business?" And she said, "Of course he's still in business. In fact his son is in the business with him, and his grandson is twenty-three already, and he's in the business too. You call him and I'm sure he'll make something for you in your price range." When I told my Mom I had ordered a jacket from him, this is what she wrote:

> *Dear Doll,*
>
> *I think you are doing the right thing by going to Walowitz. I have always been very happy with everything he ever did for me. But tell him he should give you the cost of your trips to Brooklyn, and also don't pay taxes. TELL HIM I SAID SO. Explain to Walowitz that it costs you $25 each time you come to Brooklyn, and also tell him you are not going to charge him for the time it takes you. I am not joking. He should do something for you. Remind him that he didn't give you a wedding gift!*
>
> *Love from Dad and Me*

Recently, at the conclusion of my lectures on the importance of humor, a nice Chinese man came over to me and said, "Joyce, I want you to know that having heard your mother's letters, I now know there is a universality in mothers. I also realize my mother must be Jewish!"

JOYCE M. SALTMAN

LUCY, ETHEL, AND ME

M om, listen!" *eight-year-old Meredith exclaimed,* pulling on my arm, giggling. "Lucy and Ethel are working in a chocolate factory to make some money. It's easy at first, but then the chocolate keeps coming faster and faster and faster." She stopped to take a breath. "So they're eating it, and they've stuffed their mouths *full*. And it still keeps coming. Mom!"

"I'm listening." I sighed. "But I'm trying to get ready for my presentation."

"Can I help?"

"Not tonight. I'm in a hurry." I motioned to the two black suitcases and the stacks of sample clothing—embroidered polos and corporate casual shirts— freshly ironed and folded.

"I wish you had your old job." Meredith was dressed in a nightgown, her long brown hair pulled up in a ponytail. Freckles splashed across her upturned nose as she leaned closer, dark eyes opened wide, waiting for my comment. When I made none, she stomped away to watch the old shows on *Nick at Nite*. I packed my samples and set my alarm clock, dreading the three-hour drive to my nine A.M. appointment.

My contact for the meeting had visited our facility. Together we had watched blank T-shirts rotate from station to station on the automatic textile printer while squeegees pushed a myriad of thick colored inks across the screens, making elaborate designs. Nimble-fingered seamstresses pushed cloth-cap panels beneath bobbing needles. Printers with ink-stained hands stacked sheets of paper into Heidelberg presses that cranked out newsletters that day. Wouldn't everyone like the convenience of one-stop shopping for screen printing, cap manufacturing, embroidery, and award-winning offset printing and artwork?

I thought so when I had joined the fast-growing company two years earlier. I told friends, "I have found my niche. I will write and be creative." I soon learned the company suffered from serious growing pains. My vision of producing four-color brochures and ad campaigns dissipated into selling marketing services, managing sales reps, handling production problems, and preparing last-minute sales reports for bankers. We secured national projects, but it wasn't enough. The company was sold. Now I crammed information from catalogues and price lists because there was no time to learn the intricacies that came with the day-in, day-out selling of apparel.

"You look exhausted," the receptionist said the morning after my presentation when I asked about my calls. I tried to smile. "I got the account," I said, then I dashed to my office. Inside, mounds of paperwork waited. Meredith's second-grade school picture stood on my desk. Her smile tugged at me. I missed being with her as I had been before. Had we spent enough time together lately?

I didn't have time to wonder. Employees stormed my office with paychecks in hand. One after another said, "Have you seen this?" A memo from the management attached to the paycheck said, "All employees have been assigned a number. Each employee must punch a time clock. We are presently reviewing employee health benefits."

As senior vice president, I tried to reassure them: "The new owner has the working capital to keep the business going." Inwardly, I worried. Did his plan include me?

Over the next few weeks, my assistant resigned and others found termination letters on their desks. Morale plummeted, tempers flared, and even old-timers grumbled, "It's not fun anymore." More and more accounts demanded my attention. But was it bad enough to give up my salary? With all phone lines ringing, I felt trapped in Lucy and Ethel's chocolate-factory nightmare.

Several weeks later, I returned home from a late meeting. I tiptoed into Meredith's bedroom and watched her sleep. The clock ticked. Had she grown while I was away? Nearby, my early morning note to her said, "Have fun at school. Mom loves you." After a while, I kissed her forehead.

"Mama," she said, opening her sleepy eyes, "is making a living the same as making a life?" *Out of the mouths of babes.*

The answer was easy. "No," I said, knowing the letter I would type after she was fast asleep would begin, "It is with regret that I submit my resignation. . . ."

DEBRA AYERS BROWN

A child is fed with milk and praise.
—MARY LAMB

THE I AM'S

t's not easy disciplining your children. It's one of the hardest jobs handed to any new mom or dad. Many parents today were brought up with spankings, a method our parents used to teach us right from wrong.

When my first child was nine months old, he was able to pull himself up from the floor to the coffee table and stand on his own. I thought this was absolutely wonderful. I knew it wouldn't be too long before he would be learning to walk.

But when he turned two, I found he would pull things off of the coffee table. I would smack his little fingers and say, "No, don't touch." By the time he turned four, smacking his little fingers was no longer working. I tried telling him, "Be good," but it didn't work. No matter how many times I'd repeat myself, he never seemed to listen. I sounded like a broken record: "Be still," "Don't play with the VCR," "Sit down!" "Don't misbehave at day care," and "Don't run in the street!"

In desperation, I decided to talk with my father, who, with my mother, had raised ten children. How did they do it? How did they make all of us behave? When I told my father about my son's behavior problems, he suggested, "Why not sit him down and talk to him?" This was a surprise to me because he had raised us up on spankings. I couldn't help but think that, over the years, Dad must have discovered that spankings weren't always the answer. I decided to take Dad's advice, but what should I say, and how could I change my son's way of thinking? I realized that if I could change how he thought of himself, he could change his behavior.

The next time I found myself frustrated and exhausted with my son's antics, I sat him down in his little chair, and I said, "Son, repeat after me."

> I am smart
> I am talented
> I am creative
> I am trustworthy
> I am loyal
> I am truthful
> I am athletic
> I am loving
> I am kind
> I am brilliant
> I am skillful
> I am honest, and most of all
> I am beautiful

I'm really not sure what inspired me at that moment to come up with and begin saying the I Am's. But the first time I tried it, I remember looking at my son's dear face and listening to him repeat the I Am's back to me in earnest. It made me flash back to when I used to imagine having children and wanting nothing but success for them. I saw a child that could grow up to be sensational instead of someone I didn't know. In the beginning, he may not have fully understood each word, but I could tell he understood the intent.

My son had occasion to repeat the I Am's a number of times

during his early years, and he grew to understand the meaning of each one. He's now in the fourth grade and is a straight-A student. He is a part of an after-school writing club, sings in the school choir, plays the trumpet, takes piano lessons, has taught himself to swim, and he plans to enroll in the summer league for bowling. Most of all, my son doesn't get spankings anymore.

I believe in the I Am's, and I continue to add to them often. I now use the I Am's with my two daughters as well. By incorporating the I Am's into their way of thinking, my children have learned to believe in themselves with each positive action they take.

JOY BOYD

THE WISDOM OF THE RUG

The sound of an early-morning alarm clock signals get-up-and-go or grumbling, depending on one's inner clock. As a morning lover, I perk with the coffee at 5:00 A.M. My former college roommate—one of those thrive-after-five (P.M.) types—often reminds me how irritating morning exuberance is to those who would like to skip mornings altogether.

Perhaps my love of mornings centers on a habit formed over the years. Each morning, I gravitate to my favorite quiet place, my rug. My children can attest to the care that goes into selecting the *perfect* rug, since at 5:00 A.M., it becomes my altar of spiritual inspiration, hope, prayer, and grace.

The discipline of "rug sitting" began during uncertain days in the cancer recovery process, when fear swirled like a tornado around my heart. The rug was a haven where tears flowed with abandon. The process of pouring thoughts into journal pages while sitting on the rug helped me to focus on priorities and re-arrange my future goals. Reading, writing, and listening to the Voice of Guidance led to a renewed spiritual balance.

Peace was the natural byproduct from my time on the rug. Journeying through difficult days to an oasis of calm intensified my appreciation of the simple, ordinary pleasures in life, long taken for granted before the crisis event. My health is now fully restored, but the rug remains a place of praise, pondering, and play.

Rug time allows the creativity in my work to flow freely. And rug time also allows me to be grateful—for those who have passed yet left an indelible ink print on my life, for those in the present who continue to bless my life, and for those who will decorate my future.

Several months ago, our son Chad called while traveling abroad. He said he had purchased a "memory gift" for himself. My curiosity was really piqued. When he came home with his treasure, he couldn't wait to show me. Not realizing how my rug ritual had inadvertently rubbed off on my son, I was surprised when Chad unwrapped a magnificent handwoven Moroccan carpet.

He has entrusted it to our care until it takes a special place in his home—where like mother, like son, he'll one day weave upon his own rug an even richer life.

CANDIS FANCHER

GOODBYE, EDDIE

e came out of the woods, and he must have known I was completely vulnerable. I had vowed there would never be another, but there he was, tempting me, making me feel wanted.

I don't know how I knew it, but his name just sprang from my lips. "Eddie. You're Eddie, aren't you?" I think he nodded, but sometimes it's hard to tell with cats. Anyway, he seemed to want the warm leftover breakfast oatmeal with milk and sugar. He seemed to like the buttered toast. He didn't turn down the bacon either. As a matter of fact, I never saw a cat eat that much in one sitting.

Eddie was scraggly, with that kind of devil-may-care, James Dean look. He was a guy you wanted to trust, but you knew down deep that you shouldn't. I thought all these thoughts as I reached out to pet Eddie and he turned his head up to me so that I could scratch his neck.

My beloved Kimi, a cat that lived in our house for thirteen years, had recently died. I vowed no more cats! No more attachments to animals. No more maternal responsibility to nonhumans. Then Eddie walked into my life, from out of the woods.

Eddie was a gray tomcat. He had only half his tail, and he didn't seem to mind the barrage of jokes that were directed at his very obvious defect. Rather, he seemed to flaunt his half-tail, as if somehow it was a better tail simply because it was different from most.

Whereas my Kimi ate only dry cat food from the bag, I noticed my maternal instincts moving into high gear when I found myself buying Eddie the very best canned cat food—he seemed to need it more. Whereas Kimi would jump on my lap and sit and purr as long as I would permit, Eddie directed his life on his own terms. He would much prefer to stretch out on the cool tile floor than sit on my lap. And he seemed to get along with many other animals. Kimi never could get used to dogs, but Eddie seemed to like them. Also, while Kimi used her private entrance to come and go as she pleased, Eddie preferred the back door. He preferred being let in and let out. He preferred having people do things for him.

Eddie stayed with me for a year and a half. During that time, I confided in him, but he remained the strong and silent type, the kind of guy you always wonder about. The kind who never reveals his thoughts.

Without a word, without a note, without a sign, Eddie left. I shouldn't have been surprised. I should have known that one day it would end. Maybe he was just too proud to be someone's cat. Maybe he found someone as vulnerable as I was that day he entered my life. Maybe he just got lost, like so many guys with that James Dean grin.

I'll always remember the delightful incongruity that was Eddie. He was all tomcat, but the only collar he'd wear happened to be delicate pink.

MARLENE R. JANNUSCH

LEAVING HOME:
A MOTHER'S PERSPECTIVE

blinked back tears as I gazed out the car window at a smirking orange moon. To me, at least, it seemed to be smirking, but maybe that was just my state of mind. Our car sped east into the darkness, and with each revolution of the wheels, it took me farther away from my daughter, my eldest child.

Several hours earlier, my husband and I had left her in a dormitory at Middle Tennessee State University, a twelve-hour drive from our home in Manassas, Virginia.

I had been so proud of myself as I'd said goodbye to Leah. Earlier, she'd pleaded with me not to cry—not until after we'd left her, anyway, and I hadn't. But I'd come close. As we rode down in the dormitory elevator together, Leah had been silent, keeping her eyes carefully averted from my face. I, however, couldn't stop gazing at her, trying, I guess, to imprint these last moments with her on my brain. I wouldn't be seeing her again until Christmas. My eyes lingered on a tiny scar on her forehead, an upside-down "v."

A memory flashed in my mind of a fifteen-month-old Leah pulling a clock-radio off a bedside table right in front of me. It seemed to happen in slow motion. I saw the radio falling toward her and tried to catch it, but I couldn't move fast enough. The next thing I knew, Leah was screaming, her forehead dripping blood. At the emergency room, I wept in my husband's arms, listening to my toddler shrieking, "Mommy . . . Mommy . . .

Mommy" in the cubicle next door as the cut was stitched up. Her panicked cries broke my heart, and I wished I could trade places with her. Suffer the pain for her so she wouldn't have to.

There have been many, many other times since that day that I've had the same wish—her first day in a new school when she tried so bravely to hide her anxiety, the time she didn't have a date for the homecoming dance but all her friends did, and the bleak January day in her junior year when a classmate was killed in a car accident. All those times, I wanted to take away her pain, but I knew I couldn't do it.

Just as she couldn't take away my pain as our car sped down the interstate while the miles between us lengthened and the orange moon smirked down on me in my aching sadness. But I knew my pain was only temporary. As the days passed, I would adjust to a different life without my daughter in the house.

With that adjustment in mind, I decided to redecorate Leah's room, keeping her bed and dresser but converting a section into a sewing area for me. A few weeks after we left her at college, I began to pack up the few items she'd left behind. I felt quite strong as I sifted through yearbooks, photo albums, and various odds and ends she'd collected throughout the years. But suddenly, I came across an item that shattered my emotional calm.

I picked up a green square of burlap imprinted with two small handprints in white. My eyes blurred as I read the typewritten message above the handprints, and I could no longer hold back my tears.

> Sometimes you get discouraged
> Because I am so small
> And always leave my fingerprints
> On furniture and walls.
> But every day I am growing
> And soon I'll be so tall,
> That all those little handprints

Will be hard to recall.
So here's a final handprint
To remember, Mother dear
Exactly how my fingers looked
In Sunday School this year.
                        1980

I cried unashamedly—and it felt good.

CAROLE BELLACERA

III
THE INTUITIVE EDGE

There are two worlds: the world that we can
measure with line and rule,
and the world that we feel
with our hearts and imagination.

—LEIGH HUNT

A MOTHER'S INTUITION

One day I sat on our backyard deck with two-week-old Philip cradled against my chest. Philip's two-year-old brother, Christopher, played beside me. My husband tinkered below, fixing the lawn mower.

I asked my husband to watch Christopher while I went inside. Christopher happily toddled down the stairs to his father, play mower in hand. As I watched him go down each step, satisfied that he and Dad were together, I brought Philip inside to the changing table.

As I began to diaper Philip, I suddenly felt a surge of dread and a compelling sensation that was pulling me back outside. I ran to the deck leaving Philip unstrapped and naked on the changing table—a practice I've never before or since risked.

The steep roof on our garage hangs partially over the deck. With a chair, a child can easily climb onto the roof, which is exactly what Christopher had done. By now, he was straddling the peak, one foot on each side.

I looked up just as he lifted his left foot into the air. In a split second he'd be stepping over the roof's edge and plummeting to the concrete driveway below. I let out a sound that can only be described as a wail, a bellow of pure terror.

Christopher froze. My husband ran toward us. I flew onto the roof as if I had wings, leaving my body behind. Calmly, I pulled Christopher's small body toward me and simply sat there on the roof's apex, holding him in my arms.

Only after I retrieved Philip from the nursery, and only after the four of us sat safely planted in our deck chairs, did I begin to shake.

I do not know what pulled me outside that day. I understand how adrenaline could enable me to scale the roof so rapidly, yet I cannot say what yanked me initially and insistently outside, like the tugging of an invisible lasso.

I am not a mother who takes chances. I would not have left any newborn unattended on a high table. Yet I opened to a subtle and pervasive intuitive force that exists in all mothers—just in time to save my child's life.

ANNE SPOLLEN

PALE-BLUE LETTERS

abysitting my friend's son is always an experience.
Jeb has been diagnosed with some autistic characteristics,
but it's not his disorder that gets to me—it's the way other
people react to him that can ruin my day.

Jeb is different. He isn't interested in demonstrations of affection and rarely looks anyone in the eye. If you speak too loudly,
he'll cover his ears and scream at the top of his lungs. Touch him
and he'll cry out as if in great pain.

We walk to the park every day, but not to play with other children; he doesn't enjoy making friends. He only likes hanging out
on one particular swing. He'll sway for hours, rocking back and
forth. Even though he has an expensive play center of his own in
his backyard, it's only on this one swing in the middle of the
local playground that he'll play.

Since I've been babysitting him for years, I know what he en-
joys, and I allow him almost everything that he wants: the walk
to the park, the swing, and his favorite box of crayons when we
get home in the evenings. Drawing and writing are usually how
he spends most of his nights. He invariably chooses a worn, pale-
blue crayon. Then I tuck him into bed and read to him from one
of my poetry collections until he falls asleep.

Jeb has never told me he loves me, but rarely does he get into
trouble. If he starts to get agitated in public, all I have to do is
hand him something to write with; he'll instinctively sit down
and stay busy, penning nonsensical words and doodles.

Today at the park I had a mother pull her own child away

from Jeb so the child wouldn't "catch" what Jeb has. Another father inquired, "What's wrong with him?" As always, I avoided responding.

When I brought Jeb home, I found his mother reduced to tears. She is often like this. The stress of raising a child who never shows affection tends to wear on a mother after a while.

I sat down at the kitchen table beside her. "What's the matter, Shara?"

Sniffling, she wept. "I gave some of Jeb's papers to an autistic specialist to try and figure out what's going on in his mind, what he's trying to say."

I patted her hand, thinking those scribbles and pictures weren't anything anyone could understand.

"Dr. Matovski told me the pictures were exceptional and increasingly intricate. He said Jeb's words are poetry! The letters and sentences are just backwards!"

"Really?" I gasped. "You mean the stuff Jeb writes actually makes sense!"

She gulped in ragged breaths, pulling out one of Jeb's pieces of construction paper from her purse. "Look."

I glanced down over Jeb's pale-blue crayon scribbles and noticed there were words underneath where the doctor, a pediatric neurologist, must have transcribed.

> *In the darkness I do lie*
> *Liking the quiet and the night*
> *As she reads a poem of a guy*
> *Who's not afraid of doing what's right.*

> *In my heart I yearn to be*
> *As strong as the hero's will*
> *Whose spirit was unfettered and free*
> *But whose love for women was grander still.*

Yet my love hides within my soul
Afraid to break the chains.
But withholding my emotions has taken its toll
And for my caretakers only heartache remains.

So to these two women I write this poem
To let them know how happy I am.
Their love is greater than anything I've known
And it's helping me to become a man.

—Jeb

Together, we collapsed into tears, barely able to comprehend that all this time, Jeb has been feeling fulfilled and appreciating us, loving us.

We were still embracing one another and crying when the phone rang.

"Hello," my friend answered.

"Hello, Shara. This is Dr. Matovski. I just finished transcribing the rest of Jeb's poetry. He surely has some savant abilities. Some of these are quite fascinating. Would you mind if I showed them to a friend of mine, Frank Paterno?"

"Frank Paterno?"

I heard the name and knew he owned a local publishing house.

"Sure," Shara answered. "But first send me more information explaining how you deciphered Jeb's poetry. I want to be able to read them for myself now."

"Of course, Shara. I hope you're very proud of your son. He's a very well-adjusted, talented young boy," Dr. Matovski told her.

It's been over a year since that night, and Jeb has now had two poems published in a book made to help raise funds for handicapped children. I'm not sure which his mother is more proud of, his being a poet or just being a "happy" little boy.

I believe it's the latter.

And for me, well, I remain their babysitter. We still have our daily routine of walking to the park, playing on the swing set, writing, drawing, and reading poetry at night. But now when a mother or father asks me what's wrong with him, I remember the pale-blue letters and say, "Nothing. He's perfect."

MICHELE WALLACE CAMPANELLI

*If you have enough fantasies, you're ready
in the event that something happens.*
—SHEILA BALLANTYNE

THE FORTUNETELLER

My husband and I took a short trip to New Orleans several years ago for some much-needed time to ourselves, away from our two little boys, ages seven and five. We wanted to think about the next chapter in our lives. We had enjoyed our children so much as babies, preschoolers, and now, "big boys." Soon they would both be in school, and I was thinking of returning to the world of journalism. We could certainly use another paycheck. And yet the sight of babies curled against their mothers left me with a deep maternal longing.

My husband and I checked into a hotel in the French Quarter and spent the next three days wandering through antique stores, galleries, bookstores, places that did not lend themselves to noisy little boys. We ate exotic food in quiet, candlelit restaurants and stayed out late listening to jazz. We took an eerie tour of the local graveyard and heard stories about voodoo and ghosts.

New Orleans worked its magic on me, and I found myself in a shop that sold crystal balls and special tea leaves. A sign behind the counter said that someone could see my future, if I cared to pay. What the heck. I made an appointment.

"Nancy" was a woman with long brown hair who wore a loose cotton dress that reached to the floor. She pulled aside the beads that hung in a small doorway and invited me into a room that smelled of incense. She carefully spread out Tarot cards and began to talk with me about my life. Hmmmm. She saw that I was good at the work I did. That more work was around the corner. That I would be successful. And then she stopped looking at the cards and looked into my eyes.

"Are you thinking of having more children?" she asked.

My eyes filled with water, and I felt my stomach turn over. "Of course not" was what I meant to say.

"Yes," I answered.

She'd hit a nerve, and she was pleased. "Nancy" told me that the child was wanting to be born (more tears from me) and that I could expect a girl. A girl! I thought the fortuneteller had looked straight into my heart.

My husband and I were in agreement that we weren't finished with the sleepless days of diapers, *Sesame Street,* and toys spread across the floor. The romantic setting of New Orleans was a catalyst for our decision. We returned home with a new plan for the future.

When I told my sister about my visit to the fortuneteller, she howled with laughter. "How could you have fallen for that one?" she teased.

But several weeks later, she found herself in New Orleans on a business trip with her husband. She called one night, obviously taken with the spirit of the French Quarter, and asked for directions to the fortune-teller's shop. The next day she was sitting in front of a woman with long brown hair. After some discussion, the woman said she could see that my sister was good at her profession. That more work and great success were around the corner. Then she stopped and looked at my sister. She said, "Are you thinking of having more children?"

My sister hooted at that. Absolutely not! Her kids were adolescents, and she was done with babies. Oh. The fortuneteller went on to other things, including a big move her family would make very soon. (The big move never materialized.)

Now six years later, I smile at this memory as I listen to my third son playing with trucks and blocks in the next room, alongside his two older brothers. I remember my reaction to the fortuneteller's vision, and I think: So many times, when we think we're listening to what the other person is saying, we're really listening to ourselves.

TONI WOOD

STORIES OF THE RED LAMP

Most children dread bedtime; at my grandmother's house, I cherished it. Grandma, a giant bear of a woman, would squat down beside me, take my hands in hers, and tickle the back of my skull with her intense blue-eyed gaze. "Are you and your brothers ready for bed?" she'd ask.

I would nod and run to gather my two younger brothers, then set up the three cots we slept on, nestled close together, in her living room. We spread sleeping bags over the nylon and metal beds, then climbed into the warmth, ready and waiting for Grandma to come in and tell us a bedtime story.

After a few minutes she would amble in and take her place on the scarlet couch. The intense color of the couch matched the rest of the decor well. On the floor lay an enormous red oriental rug stretching the entire length of the room. The window, framed by heavy red velvet drapes and white transparent linens, did not seem to overlook a suburban street in Minnesota, but instead opened onto a world limited only by our imaginations. In this ornate room that mimicked a Victorian boudoir, filled with the treasures of a lifetime of garage sales, the most wonderful of all the objects were the matching antique red glass lamps.

"Are you ready?" Grandma would ask, ceremoniously turning

the curled iron keys to illuminate each red glass lamp. "Do you see the path of light coming from the lamps?" Grandma would question as we snuggled farther down into our sleeping bags and squinted our eyes.

"Yes, we can see it!" the three of us replied on cue and in unison.

"Now, do you see those three little children walking on that path into the red lamp? Do you see them?"

"Yes, Grandma! Yes!"

Grandma then launched into a story of the three children—a girl and her two younger brothers—and their adventures in Red Lamp Land. Only magic, love, and peace existed in Red Lamp Land; the outside world never imposed here. We left our parents' messy divorce behind at the base of the lighted red path. In Red Lamp Land, Grandma's words soothed our fears. We three children conquered all foes, maneuvered skillfully through danger, and aspired to great heights. In Red Lamp Land, my brothers and I, working together, were invincible.

The stories about the red lamps ended a long time ago. The last time I saw Grandma, a few months ago, Alzheimer's had overwhelmed her mind and she seemed to have taken up permanent residence in the land of her own imagination. Yet I believe her to be happy; I know the world in her mind to be a rich and satisfying place. I sought shelter there myself during the most difficult days of my childhood.

In the twilight of her life, I will take her hand in mine as she readies for her long slumber. I smile as I think of her watching for the path of light that will lead her to the special place where only magic, love, and peace exist, where the outside world never intrudes. She should know the route well. She has traveled it in her dreams many times. And the children she taught to stick together, to face adversity in unison, will courageously surround her as the light dims on this world, and illuminates for her a heavenly place.

JACQUELYN B. FLETCHER

SHE'S JUST LIKE YOU

T he sun warmed my back as I stood on a snow-covered peak overlooking Squaw Valley and the deep turquoise waters of Lake Tahoe.

David's affectionate nudge in the ribs halted my meditations. "I know what that means," I replied, brushing wind teased hair from my face. "You always poke me like that when you're thinking and you want to share it with me."

"I am and I do," he said, smiling down at me. "When you get your daughter, you've got to bring her up here. I'll teach her to ski." Then he laughed and said, "Of course, since I'm also the big city boy, I'll tour the galleries with her, show her how to dress, and acquaint her little palate with only the finest cuisine. And I'd better familiarize her with the kitchen, because your cooking is utterly ordinary."

"Hey, watch it!" I said. I searched my friend's handsome face for the real purpose behind our conversation and reminded him, "Did you forget I've been disqualified to adopt a child ten times now? Even if it happens within the next few years, I'm close to fifty. Do you actually believe it will ever happen?"

"Of course I do. Look out there," he said waving a gloved hand toward the fresh pack of snow and the beautifully wooded sections of high bluffs. "That's a universal miracle—and you're a part of the universe. So, Donna, believe a child is in your future."

I cast a lopsided grin at David, wishing I possessed his natural charm and confidence and that like him, I could afford only the finest ski attire. "You are so positive, David. I gain such strength from you. And would you believe I'm the motivational speaker?"

I didn't know then, standing atop that mountain, it would be the last time we would ski together. David had a great fighting spirit, but a short while later, the HIV virus would allow disease to ravage his body. He was barely forty years old when he lost his battle with AIDS and passed on.

I never really came to terms with his death until a year later, when I visited his grave. With tears pooling in my eyes, I found myself talking to him as though we were still together on that mountain. I said, "You won't believe it, David, the most wonderful thing has happened. I've been matched up with a birth mother and father. They're going to have a baby daughter and they want me to be the mom."

In that instant, I clearly heard David's voice, as if he were standing beside me. "I know," he said, "in fact she's here with me right now. I'm telling her all about you: Your off-the-wall stubbornness, driving energy, your madcap humor, how you love sports and love to have a good time." Then I heard that contagious laugh of his. "I know patience is not your strong point, Donna, so I'll tell you now—she'll be born on June twentieth. On that date, her spirit will join her body. And Donna, she'll be just like you. She'll have your energy, your coloring, and your eyes and you two will have a laughing good time together."

I knew I had "heard" the truth from David, yet a few weeks later when I learned the date of the birth mother's scheduled cesarean delivery, June 23, I began experiencing doubt. Had I merely imagined David's graveside message?

I had almost put it out of my mind until the evening of June 20, when I answered the phone. A woman on the other end said, "Your birth mother asked me to make this call. She went into early labor and your beautiful nine-pound four-ounce baby daughter was born today at 6:06 P.M." Overjoyed, I could hardly speak. I mumbled my thanks and told her I would arrive on the first plane in the morning. David's words danced through my mind. From the bottom of my heart, I realized no matter where you find it, truth is truth.

Today, when I take my daughter to the park, or we're out together, my friends shake their heads and say, "Donna, her mannerisms and looks are incredibly you." I just smile and say, "I know. I was told she'd be just like me."

DONNA HARTLEY

All success begins with a quality decision to the vision.
—Anonymous

LOST AND FOUND

I landed at the Los Angeles International Airport at 9:20 P.M. recently after flying back from Hawaii. My feet hurt and were swollen, and I was bone-tired. I'd been having a day of mishaps, so I wasn't surprised to find chaos in baggage claim as we all tripped over one another, struggling to find our bags and get out of the airport.

Miraculously, in under an hour I'd retrieved my luggage, hailed a cab, and was home. After unpacking, I collapsed into a hot bath. It felt like heaven as I submerged myself right up to the bottom of my lower lip. I shut my eyes, drew a long breath, and let my mind drift as I let go of the day.

All of a sudden, a jolt of adrenaline hit me hard, and I bolted upright. I couldn't remember bringing my canvas carry-on into the house. I leapt out of the tub and threw a towel around myself. I tore through our house, dripping wet, looking for my little white canvas bag with the pretty blue dolphins on the side. I had bought it in Hawaii and used it as an extra carry-on. In it was a newspaper, a couple of magazines, a bottle of Champagne . . . and my jewelry! I had put my jewelry bag in it with all my priceless pieces. My diamond earrings, my diamond necklace, anniversary and birthday gifts from my husband. My black pearls that I'd gotten in Tahiti. Beautiful things, but their sentimental value was what I prized above all. Gone!

By now, it was 11:30 P.M. I frantically called the airport and got one of those infuriating recordings with a menu that led me in circles, so I hung up.

Memories streamed in of the special moments when my husband had given me these gifts, and I choked back tears. I closed my eyes and prayed to God for help. An answer came like quicksilver.

I had a vision that appeared in three distinct parts. First, I saw an angelic-looking being. A small, very old man, luminescent, with an extremely long white beard that came to a point near his waist. He was floating about six inches off the ground guarding my canvas bag. His angelic presence was so majestic that my little bag with the blue dolphins looked undeserving, even silly, sitting at his feet. Then, I saw a man's hand giving me my bag just as I had left it. Finally, I saw a clock that read 12:48. Immediately a profound feeling of peace and calm swept over me, and I knew everything was going to be okay.

The vision and warm feeling stayed with me as I drove back to the airport. I pulled up in front of baggage claim. It was oddly deserted. I looked for parking but saw only a taxi zone. I thought of how tough the parking enforcement is at LAX, but no one was around, so I took a chance and parked in front anyway.

I ran to the door and gave it a good yank. It was locked! My calm started to evaporate. I pressed my forehead against the window, searching the empty cavernous room to see if the bag was where I left it. I couldn't tell. I banged on the glass door, but there wasn't a soul around. Tears welled up. How could my vision and the calm feeling I had be so wrong?

After several minutes, an older man in a security guard uniform entered the baggage claim area. I pounded on the door again and got his attention. He ambled over and unlocked the door. I tried not to sound too panicked. "Hi. I came in on a

United flight tonight, and I left my carry-on bag by the carousel. Can I come in and look for it?"

"Oh, I'm sorry, but this area is closed," he answered. "No more baggage comin' in here tonight."

"But sir, I'll be just one minute," I pleaded. "I left it right over there." I pointed. I searched his eyes and knew he could see I was frantic. He let me in.

I ran to the spot where I had left it, but it wasn't there! My level of anxiety was increasing. "Sir, sir, could you please check in your lost and found? It's a small white canvas bag with blue dolphins on the side."

"I'm sorry, ma'am, but lost and found is closed," he replied. "I don't have a key to get in there. But I wouldn't worry about it. They'll call you tomorrow if your phone number is on your I.D. tag, or you can call—"

I quickly cut him off, "No, no, you don't understand. I have no I.D. tag on the bag. My name is not on it anywhere!"

"Oh, I see. . . . " His voice trailed off. I could tell he thought my bag was gone.

"Could you please just look in the back . . . somewhere . . . anywhere?" I said in a desperate tone.

"If it's here," he explained, "it's not gonna be anywhere except lost and found, ma'am." He broke off and sighed, knowing I wasn't going away until he looked. "What does it look like again?" he asked wearily. I described my bag, and he wandered off behind an unmarked door.

I was feeling hopeful again until my peripheral vision caught a glimpse of red lights blinking outside. I turned to see a parking enforcement officer get out of his car and walk around mine, ticket pad in hand.

I ran to the door and yelled to him, "Officer, please don't give me a ticket! I lost my carry-on bag, and a gentleman is in the back looking for it. Please, just give me two minutes. Please!" The heavyset, stone-faced officer glanced at me with complete disregard. Then, as if something changed his mind, he turned and gave me a look that appeared to be one of consideration. He checked his watch. "You've got two minutes," he stated firmly.

"Thank you!" I sang out, and I raced back inside. I scanned the area for the security guard, and came to a dead halt in the middle of baggage claim, staring at an endless stream of unmarked doors along the perimeter.

This is impossible, I thought. Nothing was going the way I thought it would. Then, out of one of those doors, came the guard—carrying my little white canvas bag! He strolled toward me as if in slow motion. The blue dolphins appeared as though they were jumping over waves as the bag swung back and forth under his grip. My heart was pounding. I looked at his hand, and just as it was in my vision, he held my bag up to me!

"Is this it?" he asked casually.

"Yes, yes it is," I squealed. I looked inside. Everything was just as I had left it. "I . . . I can't . . . thank you enough!" I said, my voice choked with emotion.

He shook his head, perplexed. "Can't imagine what it was doing back there. Shoulda been in lost and found." Still shaking his head as he sauntered away, he muttered again, "Shoulda been in lost and found."

I half-ran, half-skipped back to the car, where the officer was still hovering. "Here I come!" I hollered joyfully.

He saw me coming and laughed. "This must be your lucky day!" He smiled brightly and put his pad away.

"You have no idea how lucky, officer," I rejoiced. "Thank you!"

While driving home, I chuckled to myself as I thought about the events of the past couple of hours. How clearly I'd seen my vision, and then how easily doubts took over when things didn't look as though they were going my way.

When I pulled into our dark garage, I just sat in the car feeling totally humble and extremely grateful for the divine assistance sent my way. As I let it all sink in, I realized this was not about material possessions. My incredible vision was a gift. My lesson was trusting in the power of prayer, and surrendering to how it operates in my life.

Before I pulled the keys out of the ignition, my eyes were drawn to the clock illuminated on the dashboard. The time read 12:48.

TANNIS BENEDICT

ONE MORE CHANCE

O ne *May evening in 1986, my husband had slipped* quietly out of bed. Moments later I smelled his cigarette and heard him sobbing in the living room. I lay there in the darkness, knowing that something was terribly wrong. He had been distant for weeks now, or had it been months?

For a moment my mind drifted to a day the previous summer, to a time when it was me crying. A new stylist had butchered my hair, and I felt my precarious hold on beauty slipping away. My husband was unsympathetic. "Don't be ridiculous!" he had snapped in response to my tears. "It's just a haircut!"

That night, I felt his tears were about something much more serious. My heart was pounding when I pulled on my robe and joined him in the living room.

"Please tell me what's wrong," I said, although I feared what he had to tell me would be almost more than I could bear. My fears were justified.

"I don't want to be married to you anymore," said the man who had told me so many times before that he would love me forever. The pain was so intense I could scarcely breathe. "My feelings for you have changed," he confessed. "I don't see a future for us together." *This can't be happening. I can't let him go! I'll do anything!*

"Please," I begged through almost uncontrollable sobs, "please give me one more chance." But his mind had been made up long before tonight, and nothing I said changed the fact that my four-year marriage was over.

The years passed, and so did my fear that I could never love again. Five years after my divorce, I stood in a church and exchanged vows with my second husband. We promised to stay together until "death do us part," but in the back of my mind, I remembered sharing those vows before and how shallow those words had proved to be.

One February evening several years into the marriage, the daily struggles and arguments over money had become almost unbearable, and I had given up hope that our life together would improve. For several weeks, I had been planning how to end my second marriage.

That night I found the courage and told my husband, "We have to talk." A feeling of heaviness spread across my chest. He said he'd sensed that something was wrong. We both began weeping. In between sobs, he told me how much he loved me, and that he wanted me to be happy. With my resolve still intact, he packed his things quickly so that he could leave.

But before he left, he turned to me with a heartbroken look and said, "Please give me one more chance." I thought, *No. It's too late. Nothing will change.* But my heart heard only a haunting echo of something I had once wanted so desperately for myself.

Until that point, I thought I was certain of my path. Then something inside me shifted, and suddenly I knew I must give my second marriage the opportunity my first marriage never had. The heavy feeling in my chest lifted.

The next few years were not easy. They were filled with false starts and and many challenges as we attempted to rekindle our marriage. But I learned that love is a choice. And there were even more moments of discovery, growth, and joy than I could have ever imagined as we created our love anew.

One evening, years after the night I wanted to end my second marriage, I was deep in thought and reflecting back on my change of heart. So deep in thought, I wasn't paying attention to the task at hand—trimming my hair. With a slip of the scissors, I had a set of what appeared to me to be hideously short and crooked bangs. I had an important presentation to give the next day, and despite my efforts at "personal growth" over the years, I still cared too much about how I looked.

While tears rolled down my cheeks, I went into the living room where my husband was sitting. "I'm not beautiful anymore," I cried. He looked up at me from his magazine, and for an instant I was transported back to a summer day more than a decade ago.

But this was a different time.

The man I almost pushed away gazed at me with a mixture of love and sympathy. He then got up, took me in his arms, and gently stroked my hair.

TAG GOULET

FAMILY CONNECTIONS

flew to San Francisco recently for a speaking appearance, and my husband called me from home. Very excitedly, he relayed the events of the day.

After our daughter, Emily, left the house to see a movie with a girlfriend, a young man in her class named Adam placed a ten-foot homemade sign on our garage door that said, "Homecoming '97—Adam?" Then he lined the driveway and the sidewalk all the way up to the front door with chocolate kisses. On the doorstep he placed a red rose and a note that said, "Now that I have 'kissed' the ground you walk on, will you go to the homecoming dance with me?"

Emily got on the phone, squealed with excitement, and filled me in on the details. My first response to her: "Emily, I just have one thing to say—marry him." Now, I know she is only fourteen years old, but correct me if I'm wrong—she could do worse!

As I hung up the phone, my heart sank. I missed it! I *should* have been there! What kind of parent am I? Guilt reared its ugly head again. I flashed on the old TV series *Leave It to Beaver:* June Cleaver, dressed to the nines at all times, bustling about in the kitchen, always around when her children came home.

Left to myself in the quiet of the hotel room, I examined my "shoulds" and asked myself, *But where is the problem?* Everyone stayed "connected" in spite of my absence. Emily was floating on air. Adam succeeded—the girl had said, "Yes!" Adam's mom, who drove him to our house, sat in her car happily watching her son make his rite of passage. (Why, not so long ago, she probably couldn't get him to take a shower, and now he had transformed into Romeo asking Juliet for a date.) And my husband captured all the excitement on video. Magical moments punctuated my day in San Francisco as well. Hooking up with a dear friend for dinner capped a day of feeling very in tune with my audience, doing what I love to do.

I've discovered if we concentrate less on beating ourselves up over our self-imposed "should" list, and spend more time making quality connections with those we love, our lives will be richer.

When I viewed the situation from a "connection" point of view, I couldn't find a problem. Nothing to feel bad about.

The next week, Emily and I went out shopping for the perfect dress, matching shoes, and a slip that wouldn't show. When I told her how romantic and clever I thought Adam had been, she stopped in the middle of the mall, put her hands on her hips, looked at me warily, and said, "You're going to use this story in your talks, aren't you?"

I already had. We are so close, she knew what I'd do. I couldn't pass up a tale this good. My heart warmed, because she had me pegged. This daughter I so dearly love knows me so well that she can predict what I'll probably say or do. I realized I hadn't missed anything at all.

Like Paul Harvey wanting to relay "the rest of the story," let me tell you that they had a wonderful time at the dance, and for an evening, Emily looked like a twenty-year-old model. Unfortunately, she decided not to marry Adam. I've secretly kept his number in case she ever changes her mind!

MARY LOVERDE

IV
DIVINELY SENT

There are two ways of spreading light: to be the candle
or the mirror that reflects it.

—EDITH WHARTON

THE VOICE OF GOD

omehow my grandparents, who were raising me, had managed to survive the ravages of World War II in our native Hungary. But when that terrible war finally ended in 1945, no jubilation existed, because Soviet troops immediately held our country hostage in the arms of communism. All of a sudden, people who spoke out against these oppressions taking place were rounded up by the newly formed secret police force and never seen again.

My grandfather, a retired judge, continued to speak out freely, and in the fall of 1945, two men came to our house to get him. They said he was being taken in for questioning only. Grandfather, pointing out that his hands were dirty from working in the garden, asked if he could wash up first. The men agreed. When he didn't come out of the bathroom right away, they ran in and pushed the door open. The water in the sink was still running, but Grandfather had disappeared! He had jumped out the bathroom window and fled on foot.

After Grandfather went into hiding, life became even more difficult for Grandmother and me. We lived on soup made from the potatoes and other vegetables grown in our garden, and never knew when the secret police would show up to search our house again. Sometimes, they came in the middle of the night, breaking down the door in hopes of finding Grandfather. Fear became our constant companion, and prayer our sustenance.

For two years, my grandfather managed to elude capture, and although he sent word of his safety, most of the time we didn't know his whereabouts. Grandmother and I missed him terribly. The thought that we might never be together again plagued me constantly. But on a fall day in 1947, when I was ten years old, I knew exactly where to find him!

When new elections were held in our country, I waited for the results with great interest. The next morning our radio blared the news that the communist party had been defeated. Celebrations erupted in the streets, with none of us realizing that the communist government, backed by Soviet troops, wasn't about to give up, elections or no elections.

Certainly, after listening to the radio broadcast, my ten-year-old mind concluded the election results meant that Grandfather could come home and we could be a family again.

I wondered if Grandfather, who we recently heard was hiding out on a nearby farm, knew the good news. I decided now was the time to hike to the farm and tell him. Then we could come home together and surprise Grandmother! Of course, I didn't tell anyone of my plan. Rather than go to school, I set out on the long walk out of town to Grandfather's hiding place. As I reached the outskirts of our village without drawing attention to myself, wild anticipation filled my heart. In a short while I would see Grandfather for the first time in two years, and we would walk home together and live as a family again. My eyes filled with tears of joy with that thought, and I began to walk faster.

Startled, I suddenly heard a man's voice call my name. I stopped dead in my tracks and looked all around me, but saw no one. "Who are you? Where are you?" I asked, straining to see if he might be behind some nearby bushes.

"It isn't important where I am," the voice answered. "I'm here to warn you that you're putting your grandfather in grave danger, for you are being followed. Turn around and go back to your grandmother, immediately, and know that you will all be together again, soon."

Of course, I immediately turned and began running back toward the village, my heart pounding so hard I thought it would jump right out of my chest. I ran past a man on a bicycle and recognized him as one of the secret police. The voice had been right. I was being followed!

When I reached our house, I found Grandmother outside pacing back and forth in the street. "Oh, thank God you are all right! Someone came to tell me that you weren't in school and I thought they may have taken you," she said, gathering me in her arms.

"I decided to go and tell Grandfather that the communists lost the election," I wailed. Then I blurted out, "I thought we could come home together and surprise you!"

"Oh, my!" Grandmother shook her head.

"But a voice stopped me," I continued. "It told me I was being followed and to go back home. It was the kindest, most loving voice I ever heard, Grandmother. I believe it was the voice of God. No one else knew my plan."

My grandmother nodded, took me into the house, and held me for a long time. She told me everything would be better soon.

Two weeks later, a man came to get us in the middle of the night. By the time the sun rose, we had traveled to a place near the Austrian border where a large group of ethnic Germans were about to be deported into Austria. My heart sang when I saw Grandfather! He looked lovingly into my eyes and hugged me tightly. We were about to be smuggled out of Hungary as ethnic Germans. Recognizing the danger still around us, we didn't even breathe a sigh of relief until we crossed into Austria. There, we ended up in a refugee camp along with hundreds of other destitute refugees, but at least we were finally together.

Grandfather remained fearful that the long arm of communism could snatch him back. It wasn't until 1951, when we were given a chance at new lives in our wonderful new country, the United States of America, that he finally relaxed and lived out his life in grateful peace.

From time to time growing up, I'd wonder about the voice I heard that fall day in 1947. I'd even allow speculation when friends asked if the voice could have come from a neighbor who decided to warn me. But now, when I get very quiet and still, I know that voice, just as I recognized it as a child. Those loving, lifesaving words came from my God—the one who answers my prayers, clears my path, and lights my way.

RENIE SZILAK BURGHARDT

When circumstances seem to coincide in inexplicable ways,
the universe is reaching out to help you.
—MARY MANIN MORRISSEY

THANKS, JOE

ee-yer, getcha ice-cold beer," echoed through Yankee
Stadium. Peanuts, popcorn, and a zillion other smells
wafted over the warm summer breeze as the crowd
roared expectantly.

There was the man—long, lean Joltin' Joe DiMaggio—coming
up to the plate; an unlikely hero for a demure little girl like me.
Yet the Yankee Clipper went on to gain top spot in my personal
Hall of Fame.

Years later, our fourteen-year-old son Larry made honor roll,
became a hometown baseball star, and started avidly collecting
baseball trivia. The sport ruled his life, and everyone just knew
this kid would make it to the majors. No doubt about it.

We were a baseball family back then. Three or four evenings a
week, plus weekends, we'd all rush through an early dinner and
head out to the ballpark for games or practice.

Larry cheerfully took a job that summer that would help him
reach another goal—buying himself a ten-speed bike. In spite of
my concerns, he turned on his smiling charm and convinced me
that our Connecticut hills required all those speeds. As usual
with this lovable kid, I caved. He seemed so strong—so inde-
structible.

One afternoon, Larry took off on his beloved new bike for a quick swim before going to work. He never took that swim. He never arrived at work.

Coming down a hilly, curvy road, Larry and the bike hit a pile of sand. The bike stopped. Larry didn't. He sailed through the air, plummeted down a ravine, and hit a tree trunk—with his face.

Larry broke every blessed bone in his skull, as well as most bones in his face. Helmets for cyclists were unheard of back then.

A month or so later, after several surgeries, including a craniotomy, my boy came home. He walked into the house—a tall, bald, and disfigured skeleton—went into his room, and shut the door.

Our family's collective heart broke as the days and weeks went by. Other than visits to various doctors, Larry never ventured out. He didn't allow his friends in. It seemed as though his spirit had died.

The neurosurgeon told Larry, "No more contact sports, son, other than baseball, that is." Horrified that he would encourage my son to more risk, I questioned his reasoning. The doctor wisely explained, "While playing ball might be dangerous for Larry, to take away that part of his life could be worse."

As the months passed, I found myself wanting him to play ball, as box by box and folder by folder, Larry's baseball treasures came out of his room. "Throw these away," he'd mumble through wired jaws, "I don't want them anymore."

Late one afternoon, a close neighbor came by to see our reclusive son. As the father of his best friend, Russ passed muster with Larry and was allowed into his increasingly private sanctuary. A short while later, Larry came bounding down the hall. "Mom! Dad!" he called excitedly. "Look at this, will ya?" He held up a large autographed photograph of Joe DiMaggio. "I'm gonna show this to Jimmy and Mike." With that, he dashed out of the house and ran over the hill to find his buddies—for the first time in months.

Bewildered and amazed at the sudden turn of events, I couldn't wait to hear what had happened. We sat down as Russ, a private jet pilot for a business magnate, explained his latest flight. His only passenger that day had turned out to be Joe DiMaggio.

During the flight, Russ told the famous centerfielder all about our son. After landing, and while still on the tarmac, Joe stopped, opened his briefcase, took out a photograph of himself, inscribed, "Hang in there, kid, you can do it," and handed it over to Russ. Russ watched a single tear roll down Joe's face.

One compassionate droplet for an unknown boy's hopes and dreams—just one moment in a famous athlete's busy life—generated a glorious rebirth for our son.

Once out of his shell, Larry went on to play baseball, attend college, and marry. He now has children of his own. That photograph of Joe still hangs on Larry's bedroom wall and smiles down at him every night. Every night Larry smiles back.

LYNNE LAYTON ZIELINSKI

You shall call upon me and I will answer you. I will be with you in trouble. I will deliver you and honor you.
—PSALMS 91:15

DOUBLY BLESSED

irthing is a breeze. The toddler years, a cinch. I'm convinced the most difficult stage of parenting occurs when your teenagers begin to drive their own cars. When my twin daughters, Angela and Linda, passed their preliminary driver's education course, I found myself becoming overly anxious about potential mechanical problems and preoccupied with the dangers young girls could face while traveling alone. They, on the other hand, were full of the innocent confidence that most young drivers possess.

Shortly after getting their permits, which entitled them to drive only in Suffolk County, New York, the girls were invited to a friend's house about forty minutes away. Worried about the prospect of the girls having to travel on three different highways to get to their friend's party, I tried to talk them out of going. They were adamant about their ability to navigate the roads, however, and I reluctantly agreed. Against my better judgment, I gave them a map and anxiously showed them the routes they would need to take.

Around 2:00 P.M., armed with a credit card, the map, and instructions to call home as soon as they got to the party, they pulled away. An hour later I began to worry, and called to see if the girls had arrived. "I haven't seen them yet," their friend's mother told me, "but don't worry, I'll make sure they call you just as soon as they arrive." At 3:30, with the girls almost an hour overdue to their destination, I became frantic. Helpless to intervene myself, for the first time I called on my guardian angel and theirs to stay beside the girls and guide them home safely. My whole world felt on hold, and I could barely breathe out the prayer. But I nonetheless sought refuge in my imagined vision of angels swooping down and guiding them along a safe path. After another agonizing hour and a half, the phone rang and a timid voice said, "Mom?" I thought I'd explode, until I heard their story.

As they explained it, they got on the Northern State Parkway and never saw the sign for the first exit. They continued on the parkway west toward New York City, with Angela driving and insisting Linda read the map. Linda found reading impossible to do in a moving car and begged her sister to pull over. Afraid to pull over, Angela just kept on going! She drove right past the sign indicating they had entered Nassau County, a place where the girls' licenses were invalid, and proceeded on into Queens County. By this time, Linda became panicky. Years earlier, their grandparents had lived in Queens, and Linda knew they'd gone much too far. Yet, scared to stop, Angela continued driving.

By late afternoon, after driving through more than one construction detour, they found themselves on Grand Central Parkway. When Angela saw a sign indicating she was about to cross a bridge into New York City, she exited off the parkway instead. Now they were really lost! Their Suffolk County map did them no good, and the rush hour traffic in Queens had begun. Frightened and overwhelmed in the relentless traffic, the girls began to panic.

Spinning to look at the mass of cars around them at a stoplight, Linda noticed a red car with government plates pull up in the lane beside them. The driver, an elderly, grandfatherly-looking man, had white hair and glasses. Feeling safer because of the official tags and the driver who looked so kind, Linda rolled down her window and told him they were lost and needed to get back to the Northern State Parkway heading east. "Follow me," the driver said. "I'm going that way."

Driving slowly up ahead, he guided them from exit to exit, crossing the myriad highways, parkways, and boulevards the girls had mistakenly exited onto and off of in their fear and frustration. Finally back on the correct road, Linda and Angela followed the man until they recognized the signs they'd missed before at the correct turnoff. At that point, although neither girl saw him exit, they lost sight of the man and never saw him again.

"Linda, do you remember what time the gentleman pulled up beside you?" I asked after their return, recalling my 3:30 plea for angels to stay beside the girls and guide them safely home. "Actually, I do," she said. "I had just looked at my watch. It was exactly 3:30."

Coincidence? Perhaps. Naysayers would claim that angels are just a figment of our imagination. But I've heard that line before. "It must have been a figment of your daughters' imagination," the officer said when I called to investigate the good samaritan. "As far as I know, no red cars with government plates exist in the State of New York."

Sarah Newby

Miracles come after a lot of hard work.
—SUE BENDER

THE POWER OF PRAYER

ou will never walk again. You will have to use a wheelchair." Unprepared for the doctor's grim prognosis, I heard his words fall heavily on my ears, numbing my soul. I have always been a devotee of St. Jude, patron of the hopeless and despairing. If I had never felt hopeless before, I felt hopeless then.

My catastrophic car accident had left me unconscious and in critical condition. I awakened to find both legs swathed in casts, the left one in traction to aid the healing of a broken hip and pelvis. While I had other serious injuries, my legs were my prime concern. Working as a special-needs teacher and "on the go" by nature, I couldn't imagine being confined, let alone an invalid.

Lying in my bed motionless and relying on prayer, I wondered how I could give my ten-year-old son hope that Mom would heal. He'd been cheerful on every visit, but I saw the fear in his eyes. Looking forward to having a totally handicapped mother and the implications of that were weighing heavily on his little shoulders. He needed the ray of hope that I would not be in a wheelchair forever.

Just maybe, I thought, I could use this experience to teach what to do when adversity strikes. But I wasn't just being altruistic. I needed something besides my physical healing to sink my Irish stubbornness into—it's that trait that kept me going through the toughest challenge of my life.

It didn't take me long to become impatient with my limited mobility and even with the pace the therapists were willing to go with me. I vowed to learn everything they showed me—and then some. Attempting to move on my own at night after the nurses' last rounds, I'm sure I broke every hospital rule. I needed to make things happen my way. And being confined to a wheelchair the rest of my life didn't fit into my plans.

At first, I taught myself to move from the bed to the wheelchair. I made tiny movements for weeks, afraid of falling, but more afraid to just lie in bed. I reached a point where my arms were strong enough to swing me into the chair. Getting out of the chair and back into bed proved more difficult, but I soon developed a method of grabbing the sheets with one hand and the traction bar with the other. I wouldn't win any gymnastics competitions, but it worked. I often wondered what the nurses and therapists would have done if they'd seen me struggling on my own.

Each of my "secret" therapy sessions began with fervent prayers to my patron saint of hope, Jude. My prayers allowed me to transcend the pain as I struggled to support my weight, and I noticed my movements becoming easier. Prayers for safety and patience eventually gave way to prayers of thanks and gratitude for any little progress I made.

Once sure I could return myself to the bed from the wheelchair, I began to tackle a walker that had been left in my room by a former hospital roommate. If the nurses noticed that the wheelchair and walker were not where they had left them, they were not saying anything. I wondered if a conspiracy of silence had developed: I wouldn't say anything about my secret therapy sessions, and they kept quiet as well.

Every night in my private room, as soon as I knew I wouldn't be interrupted or discovered, I would maneuver myself from the bed to the floor, holding on to the bed rail for dear life, and slowly putting my weight on my feet. After several weeks of these ever so difficult efforts, my strength and confidence continued to build. Now came the ultimate challenge: alternating and moving my feet one inch at a time.

I had dreams of striding briskly down the halls at school, playing dodgeball at recess, and driving again—grandiose dreams to be sure, but I knew one thing for certain: there would come a day when the wheelchair would be gone and I would walk.

It came time to share my accomplishments with the person most important to me. One night, before my son arrived for his regular visit, I pulled myself into the chair and stationed the walker in front of me. When I heard him greet the nurses at the station, I dragged myself up. As he opened the door, I took a few small steps. Shocked, he could only watch as I turned and started back to bed. All of the pain, the fear, and the struggle faded as I heard the words I had longed to hear, "Mommy, you can walk!"

I am now able to walk alone, sometimes using a cane. I am able to take public transportation to shop and visit friends. My life has been blessed with many milestones and accomplishments of which I am proud. But none has ever brought me the satisfaction and joy offered by those four little words spoken by my son.

MARTHA E. NICHOLSON

YOU RANG, MY DEAR?

For years I had been besieged by almost every conceivable respiratory illness known to humankind. Pneumonia, pleurisy, and bronchitis were a way of life. My lungs routinely struggled for air, and my heart labored to pump life into me. And I sabotaged these efforts by smoking and overeating.

I'd been especially close to my father. After he died, what little sense of well-being I had vanished with the sudden onset of panic attacks. Without warning I would find my heart racing and be overcome with shortness of breath and paralyzing anxiety. I grew despondent, put on even more weight, and cried out to my now-deceased papa to help me. I heard no reply and spiraled downward into complete despair.

My aunt, a psychologist, interceded on my behalf. She coached me through my anxiety attacks and gave me the tools to begin a long journey of healing. She said the anxiety attacks were a gift, that they could teach me how to listen to myself. She repeatedly encouraged me to get quiet, go inside, and listen to my heart. For a long time, all I could hear was silence. Then, finally, I heard the sounds of a broken heart in need of healing. I shed the tears that had been blocked with food and cigarettes. I knew the pain of feeling separated from myself and Spirit. And I quit smoking and began to lose weight.

One day as I sat listening, that small still voice told me that the road back to wholeness was through prayer. I felt inadequate and unsure about praying and mumbled half-formed prayers and felt silly and embarrassed by my attempts. I decided to pray to my papa instead of Spirit. No insult intended to Spirit, but I felt more comfortable praying to one I knew better. I got out the program from my father's funeral service and read the eulogy written by my brother. He had included a wonderful quote from Edna St. Vincent Millay that captured the largeness of my papa's soul and the generosity of his heart. It read:

> *The world stands out on either side*
> *No wider than the heart is wide*
> *Above the world is stretched the sky*
> *No higher than the soul is high*

I decided to write Papa a letter. I wrote down everything that I could not speak. I told him how much I missed him, how my heart ached in his absence. I asked him to listen to my prayers and give them wings to send them where they needed to go. I cried out all my grief, all my aloneness, and all my sorrow until I was exhausted. I then fell into a deep sleep. The sound of the phone ringing awakened me. A woman from Houston whom I didn't know asked me if I had a neighbor named Paige who lived at the 306 address on my street. Bewildered and groggy, I replied that no such person lived there. She thanked me and hung up.

Just to be sure, I checked my Caller ID the next morning, certain that I'd dreamed the whole bizarre encounter. But I hadn't dreamed it at all. The memory of the call continued to nag at me as the morning progressed. For some unknown reason, I felt compelled to get the book I'd purchased the preceding day, entitled *A Treasury of Women's Quotations*. Acting on my intuition, I flipped it open, and it landed on page 306. The exact quote that my brother had read at Papa's funeral bounced back at me.

Awestruck by the simple yet profound power of Spirit, I sat down. Peace washed over me as I realized that I had, indeed, learned how to be still and listen. As suddenly as they came, the panic attacks were gone. For the first time, my heart opened wide, and a feeling of goodwill coursed through my body.

Now I pray with reckless abandon. I hear Spirit's voice, I recognize the sound of my own heart, and I never, ever screen my telephone calls!

MAGGI BOOMER

RYAN'S ANGEL

O ne warm October afternoon when I was writing at my computer at home, I heard a frantic knock on the door. My office was next to the front door, so the pounding sounded like thunder. "Lady! Lady!" yelled an unfamiliar woman's voice filled with panic.

I shot out of my chair and rushed to the door. "Come quick!" she said. "Your boy has been hit by a car!"

Ryan . . . My thoughts fused in a thousand dire images. It was impossible. He was playing in his room. He was right where any eleven-year-old should be. Safe.

Then I remembered he'd said he was going out on his bike to visit neighbors and to try to sell them the plywood Christmas yard decorations he drew, cut out with our jigsaw, and then painted. My budding entrepreneur had sold an entire "Snoopy" family to one neighbor though we'd lived in this area less than a year. Now he was making a trio of snowmen.

Visions of his sweet creations vanished as in my mind's eye I saw Ryan's body now mangled and lifeless.

Not even bothering to shut the front door, I took off running across our lawn and the empty lot that separated our house from the corner. It was a short distance, yet it was the longest span of earth I've ever crossed. Why wasn't I going faster? Why couldn't I see him yet?

I tried to scream his name but lost my voice. I felt strangely cold and numb. I couldn't feel my bare feet as they pounded over grass, then stones in the rough pavement. Suddenly, I remembered the day he was born. His first day of school. His last birthday. His smile.

I knew my life would be over if he was dead.

"Please, God, take me. Not him. Take me. I'm ready. Let him be alive. Let him be alive."

As I rounded the corner, I saw the huge Suburban and the woman driver, a neighbor I'd waved to often but had never formally met. She wasn't crying.

Her face held a stunned, incredulous look.

"Where is he?" I finally screamed at the top of my lungs.

"Mom!" Ryan's voice mercifully cut through the panic in my head.

My eyes shot to him, sitting calmly on the curb. That same stunned, glazed look in his eyes as in the eyes of the woman driver.

"You're alive!" I burst into tears. Then immediately inspected him for broken bones, internal injuries—surely something was being overlooked. As I sat on the curb next to him squeezing and poking his thin arms, I glanced at the Suburban.

There, under the back tires, I saw Ryan's twisted and crumpled bike. I realized instantly that something was very strange about all this.

"What happened?" I asked the woman driver.

"He was riding his bike between the houses and those huge bushes that hide the view of the street. But I never expected to see anyone riding a bike out of those bushes. Before I could even put my foot on the brake, he was in front of me. I hit him head on."

I looked at Ryan. Not a scratch.

"Mom, it was the weirdest thing. I saw her, I knew I was going to get hit and then . . . well, it was as if a huge hand just picked me up and put me here on the curb. I didn't touch the car at all. I sorta just flew over here."

The woman nodded. "He's so right. I know this makes no

sense. I heard his bike being crushed under my tires. I closed my eyes in horror. When I opened them, he was just sitting right there as you see him. Pretty as you please."

By this time, the police had arrived, sirens blasting, responding after one of the neighbors had placed the emergency call. The patrolman asked Ryan and the woman driver the same questions and got the same answers. Their story did not deviate in the least.

The officer scratched his head as he looked at Ryan's bike. "This is impossible! There is no way that bike could be twisted like that and your son not be dead. No way."

"Sure there is," Ryan said. "I was saved by my guardian angel."

The policeman was dumbfounded.

I smiled and winked at Ryan. We know where to look for angels and when to expect them.

So far, they've always shown up on time.

CATHERINE LANIGAN

V

BETWEEN US GIRLS

Believe it or not,
today offers you a hidden gift,
if you're willing to search for it.

—Sarah Ban Breathnach

I have enough to pay, play and give away.
—Bonnie Ingersoll

WHEN LESS IS
SO MUCH MORE

t's over. *After more than a year of arguments, anger,* anguish, tears, and lots of second-guessing, my marriage of eighteen years ended a few months ago.

In difficult negotiating, rather than split my 401(k) retirement funds, I lost everything else instead. I lost my little yellow house with its blue shutters; my pretty pine bedroom set; the honey-colored oak dining set with sheaf-back chairs; my dishes, utensils, pots and pans, blankets, towels, and picture frames; the Eureka vacuum cleaner; patio furniture, potted flowers, bags of fertilizer, the nectarine tree I planted, packages of seeds, hand tools, nails, paintbrushes, the bicycle pump, and the beach umbrella. Over the many years it took to acquire all this, each item and its corresponding memory or story were left behind in a flash.

But I wouldn't trade this grocery list of possessions for the sense of peace that has finally cloaked my tired spirit. Now that the divorce and its cold, cruel legalities are final, and my emotions and attentions are no longer so frayed, it is as if someone hit the restart button on my synapses.

My five senses have suddenly intensified. Colors look dazzling;

food tastes delicious; scents smell wonderful; silk and flannel, cool water and warm hands feel good to my skin; and the voices of the people I love sound like music.

And with this reawakening comes gratitude for a new start—and for the houseful of worn-out, castoff possessions I so easily acquired in the whirlwind course of about a month. Many items were generously donated by helpful, concerned friends. Others were found on the side of the street with "Take Me" signs attached to them.

In the living room, an afghan covers the worn upholstery on the small piece of sectional couch I found (who knows what became of the rest of the couch?), and a blue woven shawl disguises a rather ugly rocking chair. My beloved books, which used to rest on solid oak shelves, now are roughing it on my new bookshelves of stacked bricks and plywood—home sweet dorm.

The dining room set is a round coffee table with four pillows around it that I hand-picked out of an apartment building Dumpster. I washed and resewed the covers, and my daughters and I kneel on them like a Japanese family. None of the dishes or silverware match. Neither do the place mats and cloth napkins inherited from several sources.

In the kitchen, the refrigerator is harvest gold, bought at a secondhand store for $49. My used frying pan lost its nonstick coating at least 500 meals ago.

My two daughters, who divide their time evenly now between two houses just a block apart, sleep on hand-me-down frameless mattresses. I covered the warm but stained garage-sale comforters with new cotton duvets, and the girls hung up their posters and school artwork and set up their critter cages to complete their bedroom.

There's joy in this mishmash of throwaways. These possessions have stories, but they are not mine. There's no emotional attachment; I could toss them as easily as I found them. There's a freedom in that. And it's all I need right now.

Did I decide to leave the marriage lightly? No way. But having lived under a marital roof of joyless rigidity, barbed negativity, and frequent criticism, without any hope of improving, I realized I couldn't live in that loveless environment any longer. I'm grateful for the chance to be a role model to my two daughters. I know they will slowly begin to understand that staying in an emotionally abusive relationship isn't healthy.

Suddenly, I see choices, possibilities. I'm nearly giddy with anticipation about what direction to take my life in. I can travel to any country, learn any language, or join any club. I can think my own thoughts and then bounce them safely off close friends. I can dance in the street, sing at the market, burp in a restaurant, giggle in church, eat chocolate in bed. I can leave dishes in the sink for two days. I can acquire brand-new possessions—or not. They seem so unimportant at this point.

It's the strangest feeling: I'm in debt up to my earlobes with legal fees and now must struggle weekly to live within the confines of a single-income household. I've lost everything I ever bought in the past eighteen years. Yet I feel rich. This is not just Pollyanna prisms-and-glad-games sentiment. I'm beginning to understand how regaining control in one's life offers a wealth beyond measure.

It's really not so awful losing so much. My spirit has just landed a windfall.

KARIN ESTERHAMMER

THE REUNION

The girls were getting together again. I greeted the
invitation to a reunion with my friends from high
school with feelings of apprehension as well as anticipation.

We had been closer once. Some members of the group moved
away, but seven of us had managed to stay together all through
high school. Even though we might've had different interests, we
shared the same commitment. No matter what, we wouldn't follow fads or fashions—favoring comfort, we preferred flats when
stilettos were in style. We watched *60 Minutes* more avidly than
we watched *American Bandstand*, and enjoyed plays more than
sock hops. Some of us even read poetry. We would stay true to
ourselves. This commitment formed a bond between us and
helped us survive our adolescence.

After high school, some of us got together, now and then, for
lunch or dinner, sometimes bringing along the men in our lives.
Eventually, family and career demands beyond our control made
our times together rare treats instead of frequent habits. Months
became years. We were slowly becoming strangers. This invitation provided a chance to rediscover the friends who knew me
when I was most innocent and most vulnerable.

We met for lunch at a restaurant where my friend Marianne's
daughter worked. How could a friend of mine have a daughter
that age? I still felt like a teenager myself when I managed to
look beyond the lies the mirror told.

We were all on time. Even me. Finding clocks superfluous

when we were younger, I never seemed to be at the right place at precisely the right time. The years had managed to work a few miracles.

We spent the first few minutes noting the most obvious changes in one another: new hairstyles, eyeglasses, pounds gained and pounds lost. After we sat down, there followed an obligatory exchange of wallet photos, inquiries about husbands, children, parents. As the photos passed through my hands, I began to wonder whether this meeting was such a good idea. Maybe there had been too many changes in our lives.

Some of us were married. Some were not. Some had children, others did not. We worked in totally different fields, lived in different neighborhoods, different worlds.

But, by salad time, I could see, despite the intervening years and the changes they brought, we were still the girls and very much our own women. Although our lives had followed different patterns, we still had the same values.

We talked about our own work and special interests more than home or family, because at this stage in life, we finally have time for ourselves. We were at quite an intense point in the conversation, trading experiences in our battle for equality in the workplace, when in came the waiter with balloons for Margaret. My friend's surprise birthday party reminded us more than ever that we were, after all, just girls wearing the masks of women.

Just girls, sharing birthday cake and chocolate mousse, moaning about the calories as we sang "Happy Birthday" to our friend and, at the waiter's request, to the party at a neighboring table.

For a moment, I caught a whiff of the butterscotch brownies we used to eat on Saturday afternoons in my friend Mary's kitchen so many years ago.

The time seemed right to bring out our treasured memories, hold them up to the light of our laughter, and examine them once again, like the rare jewels they are.

The past came to life. We relived a trip to the Sands Motel, a weekend rehearsal for adulthood where we giggled our way through dinner at the Polynesian Room of the old Edgewater Beach Hotel in Chicago and an all-night pajama party. The following day, we rode the bus home, wearing leis around our necks and world-weary expressions on our faces.

Memory followed memory. We relived afternoons spent playing the card game Spoons. We relived early parties with boys who used forks as weapons, catapulting pieces of chocolate cake across the room at us. Boys who played weird sound-effects records of bombs exploding that never failed to wake my baby sister. Boys who later danced with us to the theme from *A Summer Place.*

The past had never been more real. As memory played games with reality, I saw age as nothing more than smoke and mirrors after all. No matter what superficial changes time might bring, we would always be the girls.

MARY SASS

You never get over bein' a child
long's you have a mother to go to.
—Sarah Orne Jewett

THAT "KODAK" MOMENT

Life is full of photo ops. I tried to be the good mom and take pictures of all those "special times"—birthdays, the prom, graduation, and so on—but I think I missed the boat. It's funny how the most vivid memories I have in my own mind of the years spent raising my two boys are not these kinds of moments.

I don't remember birthdays much. After the first birthday for the first child, the pictures all began to look alike, the memories all run together. Proms, the big game, Christmas—these were all great, and they're recorded for posterity in our photo albums, but they are not the times I remember best. No, the really significant occasions, good and bad, the ones I remember best, are unfortunately not on film. I just have never been camera-ready when the real events happen.

One of those "Kodak" moments caught me by surprise last Saturday morning. At about 11:00 A.M., I took a ride into town, and on my way, I decided to stop by my son Will's apartment to drop off some of my homemade spaghetti sauce. Most of the guys were at work except Will's roommate, Jeff, and my eighteen-year-old, Curt, who still lives at home but had spent the night at his brother's. "Curt's still asleep, and he doesn't feel well," Jeff told me.

I tiptoed into the bedroom and noticed a fan blowing directly on a mound of rumpled bedding.

"Curt?" I ventured.

From the middle of the bedding a voice croaked, "Mom?" Then a long pause. "Mom, I'm really sick."

"What's wrong?" I asked, going to the bed.

"I've been puking since early this morning. I even puked blood." That didn't alarm me. Curt has always thrown a little blood into his stories for dramatic effect. His head, eyes closed, emerged from the sheets, then dropped back down.

"I think I have to puke again." I wasn't born yesterday. I knew that sour smell that permeated the room. I asked him a couple of pointed questions.

"What did you drink last night?"

He hesitated, knowing how I felt about drinking, but realized denial was pointless. "A couple of beers."

"How much is a couple? A couple of pints? Quarts? A six-pack? A case?"

"I had about four beers. I swear, that's all I had." When Curt swears to something, I've learned to at least double or halve what he swears to, as the situation calls for.

"Then you went to bed?"

"No. I had the beer about midnight. I went to bed around two A.M. I felt fine," he groaned.

"How long did it take you to drink these four beers?"

"About an hour."

This conversation, translated into "Curt talk," told me that he had drunk somewhere between eight and twelve beers between midnight and 2 A.M. No telling what he downed before then. I realized that I would never have known anything about this if I hadn't made an extra-large batch of spaghetti sauce that morning.

I wanted to shake Curt and yell, "How many times have I warned you and your brother about drinking? How many times have you been told how dangerous it is—how it can suck you in? How dare you endanger yourself so carelessly after your father and I, who love you both so much, have invested all we have in you? After we've taken such care to keep you safe and healthy for the past eighteen years?" At the same time, I wanted to gather his rancid self into my arms and tell him about my relief that he hadn't ended up in the hospital or worse. I felt grateful that he would survive this lesson.

"You have a hangover," I said matter-of-factly.

"I don't think so. I feel awful, Mom. I must have the flu or something. It's really bad."

"It's a really bad hangover." I felt his head. He had no fever. I got a cold rag and put it on his closed eyes. "It's not the flu. It's a hangover. You've poisoned your system. That's what a hangover is. I hope you will remember this."

We sat there quietly. I stroked his hair. "Mom, I feel so bad I just want to cry. I'll never forget this. I'm glad you're here."

Definitely a "Kodak" moment.

I wish I'd had my camera.

LILLIAN QUASCHNICK

SECOND WIND

April days in Portland, Oregon, can convince you that winter will never end. A gray sky of drizzle after two weeks of downpours and puddles in the parking lots wouldn't give way. Looking at the city through the trees, I sat at my desk feeling a little sorry for myself. It seemed like I'd been giving out so much for so long. Juggling the multiple priorities most professional women do, I felt tired and discouraged.

I noticed the clutter on my desk: clean-up from a business trip piled high, stacks of articles, projects that needed attention, and an overwhelming list of phone mail messages. Slumping in my chair, chin in hands, I wondered what all this was worth.

The physical, emotional, and spiritual energy required in a field that called upon my professional singing, speaking, and consulting talents was exhausting. Giving out to others in an effort to make a difference had taken its toll. I wondered, *Does any of this really matter? Am I making any kind of contribution?* My thoughts turned to prayer. *God,* I thought, *You wanted me to do this, and I don't think I'm helping anyone. Maybe I'm just fooling myself!*

Morosely, I was plotting the career change I would inevitably need to make when the phone rang. The ring startled me from my brooding. A lyrical male voice, obviously Southern, said, "Hi, I'm Dan, and I'm calling from Texas. You don't know me, but I heard you sing in Japan."

Japan! That was years ago. It seemed like another lifetime. "Well," he continued, "I figured I needed to call you, because your music made a real impact on my life, and I figured you don't always get to know. I heard you sing at that school for missionary kids in Tokyo. During your concert, I was so moved, I knew then and there I needed to change direction. After your concert, I started studying my music so I could go into the ministry myself and touch others the way you touched me. I'm calling you because I just graduated from college this week and will be moving ahead with my dream."

"How in the world did you even find my number?" I asked, fairly stunned at these revelations from this friendly stranger on the end of the line. "Oh, I called around till I found it," he said. "Somehow, to call you right now felt real important."*Real important!* Little did he know!

We continued with our conversation, remembering that day years ago when I sang and spoke in Tokyo. I remembered feeling scared out of my wits singing for an assembly of high school kids. He remembered several of the songs. I remembered thinking it had probably been a total waste. He remembered it changed his life! As we exchanged addresses, I realized God had used the telephone to "reach out and touch someone." I don't always get to know whom I touch or how. I don't always get to know the impact when I give of myself. I don't always get to see the fruit of my labors. But this time, God used his impeccable timing to give me a precious gift—a call from a young man named Dan to give me a second wind.

KAREN HOWELLS

STRAIGHT TO THE TOP

I *finished ushering the last fan out of the ballpark in* Arlington and turned to my supervisor. "I need to speak with the president, please," I said. The supervisor looked at me dumbfounded, so I repeated: "I need to speak with Tom Schieffer, the Texas Rangers' president." With a smirk he let out a hearty chuckle and explained that no one at my level talked with the president. Now I looked baffled. "Do you mean to tell me that the Rangers' president won't talk to one of his own employees, an usher?" I asked. Rolling his eyes, my supervisor rattled off a canned speech about how busy the president is, running a ball club and all. "Mr. Schieffer," my supervisor said, "trades players, signs sponsors, and evaluates ticket sales, among other things. He doesn't have time to talk to people like you." Now I laughed heartily.

Long ago I learned from my mom that if you have a good idea, you need to share it with others. I told my supervisor that I believed in taking those ideas straight to the top, with or without him. "Usually the person in charge is happy to listen to positive ideas that will uplift the spirit," I stated passionately. My supervisor folded his arms over his chest, and firmly informed me I could not speak with anyone, let alone the president. Feeling patronized, I whispered, "We will see about that" to the now empty ballpark.

The next day I sent my first idea straight to the top. My supervisor could perhaps prevent me from talking with the president, but no one could stop me from mailing my ideas to him.

I wrote Mr. Schieffer a note, explaining that I found the employee break room to be uninspiring, with its stark white walls. Six hundred seasonal employees took turns retreating to that room for a breather after they worked a number of scorching innings. Knowing a problem should be addressed only with a solution in mind, I created a number of vivid, inspirational posters designed to remind employees of the magic that comes from being a part of the Rangers franchise. Folding the posters and my letter into a large envelope, I addressed them directly to "Tom Schieffer, Texas Rangers President."

The next day, I arrived to find the break room buzzing with energy and laughter. My colorful posters adorned the walls.

Over the next few months, I frequently sent Mr. Schieffer poems I composed about the ballpark. My themes touched on the entertaining and compelling ritual of baseball: winning a game against our archrival, watching a father take his son to his first game, losing a teeth-clencher. I always signed the poems with my name and title: Marguerite, The Usher.

Late that summer, I arrived to work one day and received my daily assignment: I would be working in the owner's section. That bright sunny afternoon, I passed Mr. Schieffer's seat. "Marguerite, The Usher," he read from my name tag. "Are you Marguerite, The Poet?" Laughing, I confessed and explained that I had many ideas he might like to hear, and could we arrange a meeting? With a smile, he quickly agreed.

Several meetings later, Mr. Schieffer expressed his appreciation for my positive attitude, hard work, and inspiring ideas. He then asked if I'd like to "go straight to the top" and offered me a position as his executive assistant.

This past year, Mr. Schieffer and I have shared many ideas while working together to create a positive, upbeat attitude at the ballpark in Arlington. When anyone shares an idea with me, regardless of whether they are an usher or a vice president, with a bold smile I tell them to go *straight to the top!*

MARGUERITE MURER

MAGGIE

I watched the old woman struggle down the sidewalk, her shoulders hunched, her back bent. She lurched awkwardly behind her walker, and as I approached, I saw her lined face and thinning gray hair. A teenager on a skateboard zipped by, exuding youth and vitality. "Look out," he yelled as he brushed against her. The old woman turned her head away in anger, but I saw the glint of tears and the lost look of the old and unloved. And I thought of Maggie.

I never knew Maggie's age or what kind of life she'd had before I met her. Certainly, she bore the marks of a long, hard life of ill treatment, and she had a certain way of flinching whenever somone moved suddenly.

I hadn't planned to bring Maggie into our lives. I took the children to Valean Farm to look at donkeys, not buy one. But one look into the dark-lashed lustrous eyes gazing with childlike curiousity into mine undid all my resolve. I wanted one.

We chose a lively colt whose soft muzzle poked inquisitively into my pockets, looking for a treat. Small and neatly built, Lexy stood no higher than my shoulder.

"She'll want a companion," said Val, the owner. "Donkeys don't like to live alone."

My face must have shown the dismay I felt. If one donkey stretched our budget, what would two do? "I don't think we can afford two," I said with a lump in my throat, mentally bidding Lexy goodbye.

"Well, I can see Lexy'd have a good home with you. Tell you what I can do. I have an old donkey here, too old for driving or hauling anymore. I took her on a trade and to tell you the truth, she's not much to look at. Can't get anyone to buy her, and I don't want her. But she has a gentle nature, and if you like, I'll throw her in with Lexy. She's over there."

I followed Val's pointing finger. A gray donkey stood alone, aloof from the other donkeys still crowding around us. Even at a distance, I could see that her coat was rough and patchy, with dark skin showing through here and there. "Don't mind the coat," continued Val. "She has a touch of the mange, but it'll grow back in soon."

We walked over to her. With coarse hair, sparse lashes, and ears that were scabbed and black from the mange, she looked even worse close up. She had a heavy build, with none of the grace of the other donkeys. She didn't look up as we approached, making it patently clear that she had no interest in us.

"Her name's Maggie," said Val. "She's broke to ride and she doesn't mind the saddle. Here, I'll show you." Val pulled a saddle off the fence and strapped it on Maggie. Maggie stood quietly, still not looking up. "Hop on." Val lifted up my son Nathan, plopped him on Maggie's back, and slapped her rump. Maggie walked a few paces, looking neither to left nor right. "See?" said Val. "Gentle as can be, and nothing spooks her." Maggie turned and came back toward us. For a moment, our eyes met.

And in her eyes I saw resignation and despair. Maggie knew that she wasn't lively and young like the rest of the donkeys around her. She knew that she wasn't wanted or desired, that she had no beauty or grace. And she knew that she was going to spend the rest of her life handed from one uncaring owner to another.

I walked over to her, put my hands under her grizzled muzzle, and lifted up her head. "Maggie," I whispered, looking into her eyes. "You're coming home with me. I'm going to give you a warm barn with lots of hay, fresh water, a green pasture, and an apple tree to give you shade on hot, sunny days. And I will take care of you for the rest of your life."

Maggie and Lexy arrived the next day. Lexy bounced out of the trailer and galloped up and down the fields, exploring every nook and cranny of her new home. Maggie walked over to the corner of the barnyard and put her head down. I understood. She'd been disappointed so many times before in her life. She knew better than to trust the whispered words of a stranger.

It took many months before Maggie allowed herself to enjoy her new life. She eventually came to have her favorite spot under the apple tree, her own corner of the pasture where the new grass grew tallest, and her own place in the warm, hay-scented shelter of the barn. Maggie learned to be loved—to lift her head for a special scratch under her pendulous lower lip, to lean gently against my side so that I could slip an arm around her neck, and to nuzzle in my coat pocket for the special treat she knew I always carried. She looked up at the sound of my voice, and in her own cumbersome way, galloped down the side of the hill to meet me. She joyfully brayed a welcome through the barn when I appeared in the mornings, and snuffled a wet goodnight into my ear as I closed the door at night.

Maggie knew she was loved—not for how she looked or for what she could do, but just for being Maggie.

She died in the spring six years after she came with us. She died in her corner of the pasture, with a wisp of new green grass in her mouth. She died quietly, without fuss, as she had lived her life. But in a departure from how she had lived most of her life, Maggie died loved.

For the old, the unloved, and even the unlovable, Maggie is my reminder that love is a one-way flow until the heart learns to trust.

PATRICIA WILSON